Greek Mythology

Greek Gods, Goddesses, Heroes, Heroines, Monsters, and Classic Greek Myths of All Time

By Lance Hightower

Table of Contents

Introduction

When we think of the best stories of Ancient Greece, we naturally think of the Heroes and the trials they faced at the hands of the Gods and Goddesses who ruled from the heaven of clouds high atop Mount Olympus. Hercules, Perseus, and Jason and the Argonauts have all thrilled us with their strength and courage, their adventures and their indomitable spirits, but there's more to these stories than what's portrayed in movies and children's books.

The stories live on because they represent man's fascination with immortality; the circle of consciousness to which man's attention has always been turned and his need to believe there is more to existence than what we experience on Earth. They represent our belief that we are close to the edge of creation and all we need to do is lift the veil to witness the secrets, that we can communicate with our universe and perhaps control it; we may even find out we are equal to the gods.

The ancient Greeks, with their infinite imaginations, gave us stories about their world, each one a microcosmic look at how integral their gods were to their society and the complex position they held in the human experience, how they gave form to society's ideas about the sacred and the secular, about exclusion and inclusion, about age, beauty, sexuality, privilege and status, life and death, courage and immortality.

Religion and worship in some form has probably always been part of man's history. Whether that worship was directed at the seen, the unseen, the known or the unknown, cultures across the world have generally worshipped something or someone.

For the ancient Greeks, the bridge between man and his gods was never vague. They worshiped directly, speaking to the gods as openly as they spoke to anyone, or through beasts or animals who guarded sacred oracular sights and who were said to be the "voice" of a particular god. In fact, gods and goddesses often took human form and even mated with humans to create hybrids – "humans" who were part man (or woman) and part god.

Virtually every conceivable area of life and physicality was covered by one god or another, and some of the names of these gods and humans remain part of our modern vernacular. A person might be referred to as a Narcissist or might perform a Herculean feat of bravery.

And just like a game of cards in which there is always a trump, when it came to the gods, the nature of a particular domain and even their lineage decided who held the trump. In other words, there was a hierarchy of gods just like there was a hierarchy to a line of kings. People believed that the gods controlled their lives in all things whether it was a crop failure or a blessed marriage. Authorities, priests and kings of men held societal trump cards and declared themselves the liaison between men and the gods. In many cases, they believed themselves to be ordained to their position by the gods and were therefore all powerful. Some even believed themselves to *be* gods.

But as you will see, the Ancient Greek Gods would not be trumped by any man, at least not the way the legends tell it.

These stories tell us about their world – the world of Gods and Men – a world where everything was controlled and created, including the weather, the sun, the waters, the forests, and the animals – by gods. The Ancient Greeks believed that every mountain, river and rock was either a god or contained a god or goddess. And many stories explain how parts of our modern beliefs came to be. The ancient world was alive with the imaginations of men!

In those days, it was believed that the Immortals were not much different from mortals except on that one point. They were born of a mother and father, had children and families, and lived in a home, but they were immortal and controlled everything, while men were mortal and had control over very little. Gods were stronger than men, with the exception of heroes like Heracles and Perseus. But Heracles and others like him were part God, conceived by the union of a god and a human and were shown much favor by their godly parent.

The ancient tales include confrontations with horrifying beasts who would test our heroes and be challenged by them, and with some assistance from the gods and goddesses who showed them favor, they would overcome the monsters, sometimes with the help of magical weapons and sometimes by the bewilderment or enchantment of the enemy.

The drama that unfolds on Mount Olympus, home of the gods, seems a world away from how we live today, but the stories still fascinate us. They shaped the way this ancient society lived, its understanding of Nature and war, of relationships and power. The Ancient Greeks, who cultivated some of the most superior minds of the time, believed these gods really existed in the same way members of today's religions believe what they believe.

Nevertheless, classical literature relates these stories as the invincible truth as it was believed in those days. Their heroes achieved victory against all odds and the ageless tales were examples of how to live, how to behave and how to worship. They're filled with life lessons, morals and values, and the gods and goddesses, demigods and heroes, monsters and creatures all had experiences that people could relate to; experiences that would show them the consequences of lying, cheating, killing, or stealing.

Still other stories demonstrate the bad behavior of gods who often lived without consequence for their actions. Their leadership was often questionable and their vices many, and they could be taken to task by their peers.

But the mythical characters still entertain and inspire. They teach the value of courage, love, loyalty, strength, perseverance, leadership, friendship, and self-reliance, and the consequences of jealousy, greed, deceit, lust, hate, ambition, and treachery.

Like all stories and legends that have been handed down through generations, some stories conflict in the telling, with characters and events being described in different ways. Many stories are mixed with real historical events, making them all the more believable. Others seem as fantastical to us today as a Disney movie. But each reflects the culture of that portion of humanity we know as Ancient Greece and shows us their fears, courage, frailty, and determination as well as every other aspect of their spirit – the spirit that is the worst and best of mankind.

Chapter 1: In the Beginning

All creation stories must have a beginning and this one begins in Chaos. This is the story of how the world began in a void of nothingness that swirled and collided in the dark; invisible and dumb to the senses. And like all creation stories, there is a lot of confusion, misinterpretation and...well...chaos. The most popular stories and orders of deities are presented here as they've been written in the ancient texts of Hesiod, Plutarch, Homer and others; the scholars of the time.

From Chaos, the Void, were born Erebos, who was the personification of Darkness, and Nyx, who was the Night, the mother of Sleep and Death, said to be a primordial being of such exceptional power and beauty that she would be feared by all the gods to come. Both were formed from nothing but the desire to become form. Together, they created order from chaos and so began the lineage of the world.

Aether, who was the Upper Air, what we might call the stratosphere, was Heaven, and his pure essence was unavailable to be breathed by humans. He was the Light, born of Darkness (Erebos) and Night (Nyx).

Hemera was the Day, sister to Aether, though she is said by some to be the daughter of Chaos and Nyx, not Erebos and Nyx.

Here's a look at some of the words of the playwright, Aristophanes, written in 414 BC. This bit of text from *The Birds* will give you a better idea of how these beliefs may have taken hold. The words in brackets have been added for clarity.

"At the beginning there was only Khaos [Void], Nyx [Night], dark Erebos [Darkness], and deep Tartaros [Hell Pit]. Ge [Earth], Aer [Air] and Ouranos [Heaven] had no existence. Firstly, black-winged Nyx laid a germless egg in the bosom of the infinite deeps of Erebos, and from this, after the evolution of long ages, sprang the graceful Eros [Love] with his glittering golden wings, swift as the whirlwinds of the tempest. He mated in deep Tartaros with dark Khaos, winged like himself, and thus hatched forth our race [the birds], which was the first to see the light. That of the Immortals did not exist until Eros had brought together all the ingredients of the world, and from their marriage, Ouranos [Heaven], Okeanos [Ocean], Ge [Earth] and the imperishable race of blessed gods [Theoi] sprang into being." – Aristophanes, *The Birds*

One early philosophical thinker, Pherecydes, believed there were three divine principles that existed from the beginning, Zas (the prototype of Zeus; sexual creativity), Chthonie (Earth) and Chronos (Time), and that from these all life was formed.

"Once Chronos, alone and without a partner, cast forth his seed, and from this he made fire, air, and water, and deposited them in the five hollows from which arose another generation of gods. The fiery gods dwelt in

Ouranos and gleaming Aether, the gods of wind in gusty Tartaros, the watery gods in Chaos, and the gods of darkness dwelt in black Night. Then Zas became Eros and married Chthonie, who became the wedding gift given her by Zas; she became the gift and was called Ge, the Earth.

"But below the Earth, in a hollow of Tartaros, Ophioneus was born. He and his monstrous sons challenged Kronus, that whosoever should fall into Ogenos [hell] would lose the battle and the other would possess Ouranos [heaven].

Here we see Kronos mentioned, but he is not the same as Chronos or Time (Father Time) which was part of the Void and which sprang from nothing. This Kronos is the offspring of Ge (Gaia) and Ophion (or Ouranos in most writings).

"Zeus honored the victorious gods and assigned them their domains. Kronus had won Ouranos, the Heavens. These are the shares of the other gods: below Ouranos is the fiery

Aether; below Aether the portion of Earth; below that portion is Tartaros which will be guarded by the Harpies, the daughters of Boreas. There, souls are borne through the portals and gates of Tartaros on an outflowing river to birth; the river is like the seed that leads to new life. And the souls of men depart from life and enter again the caves and hollows of Tartaros through its portals and gates. Alongside Tartaros is Chaos and the realms of dark Night."

Here the writer alludes to the fact that we (humans) might be given an opportunity to be reborn as "souls are borne...on an outflowing river to birth"; to another human life, perhaps to grow the soul or do better the second time around. But as you can see, there is no much discrepancy among the ancient writers and philosophers, but all creation stories seem to follow the same path; the world was created from nothing (a void) from which came the elements who bore the gods that eventually created and ruled the world of men.

The Protogenoi: The First Born Gods

The Immortals of Ancient Greece can be categorized into several groups, with the Protogenoi being the first born gods or the First Class of Immortals. They were the original Immortals from which all other gods came, who eventually began the race of mortal men who were sometimes enemy, sometimes friend and sometimes lover to the Immortals.

These beings emerged from the primordial ooze, from Darkness and Night, to become the fabric of the ancient universe, each personifying and embodying their element, and later, in the age of men, appearing in anthropomorphic shapes. Each successive generation of gods would take on the attributes of their parents and more, so you will find that the title God of the Sea, for example, is attributed to more than one god, some greater, some lesser.

These are the generations of Protogenoi, the primordial gods, the elements who came from Aether and Hemera: Pontus, Thalassa, Ouranos (Uranus), and Ge (Gaia), who were born without coupling.

Pontus was the primordial Sea God, whose name means "the road" because in the days of Ancient Greece, the sea was the road to everywhere. He is said by some to be a son of Gaia, not Hemera, and from him came Nereus (the Old Man in the Sea), Thaumus who was the sea's powerful dangers, Ceto, and Phorcys.

Thalassa, the Sea Goddess, who together with Pontus, bore all sea life (Oceanids). She is the mother of the Nine Telkines by Pontus and also of Halia, the personification of the saltiness of the sea and the wife of Poseidon.

The Telkhines have been variously described as being identical to the Hekatonkeires (Storm Gods) and Elder Cyclopes (Metalworkers) because they were said to have invented the art of metalwork. They were responsible for creating the sickle Kronos used to castrate Ouranos and the magical trident of Poseidon.

"From the briny deep of Pontus, she [Thalassa] bore the smiths, whose gift was concealment [magic] and who would be appointed by Gaia to raise Poseidon. The sorcerers had eyes that brought on hail, rain, snow and all manner of destructive weather, yet worked with brass and iron to reduce the lust of Ouranos by Kronos and forge the mighty trident of their charge, Poseidon."

Uranus (Ouranos), the first son of Gaia by Aether. In those days, there was little known about the universe, and the Ancients thought the world was a vast flat expanse covered by a dome that protected them from falling off the earth. Ouranos was Sky Dome, and his consort and mother was Gaia, the earth.

Gaia, who was Mother Earth, the Goddess of Land, arose from the earth, gave birth to the earth and was the earth all at once. She is therefore seen as one of the most important of all the deities and the seat of the generations of gods to come. Unlike later generations of gods, the primordial gods were inseparable from their element and were not viewed as a personification of that element.

The Ancient Greeks (as well as the Romans, Norse and just about every other ancient civilization) perceived these primordial gods in two ways: As an element or object (sky, land, sea, air, volcano, storm, sun, for example) and as the personification of that element. We can look at this in the same way we might view ourselves; we are a living person and also a spirit, which some call the soul, that gives our human body life. So Gaia, for example, who was the earth, was also in the earth and could be seen as a figure/god who represented and ruled the earth.

Hekatonkheires, Cyclopes and Titans

With Uranus, Gaia bore the Hekatonkheires, the Cyclopes and the twelve

Titans who would eventually give rise to the next generation of gods - the Olympians.

The three Hekatonkheires were enormous creatures with fifty heads and one hundred arms of immense strength. They were skilled at fashioning weapons made from earth's resources. The three Cyclopes, Arges (thunderbolt), Steropes (lightning) and Brontes (thunder), also called the Elder Kyklopes, are so named for their one round eye which appeared in the middle of their forehead. These six Immortals were feared by their father, Uranus because they were wild, lawless and unpredictable, so he had them imprisoned in the underworld, Tartaros, the bowels of the earth.

The Titans were the third set of offspring created by Gaia and Uranus, called the Uranides: Kronos, Oceanus, Iapetus, Hyperion, Crius, Coeus, Rhea, Tethys, Theia, Phoebe, Themis and Mnemosyne. From Iapetus came the four Iapetionides: Atlas, Prometheus, Epimetheus and Menoetius.

Eurynome and Ophion (Ophioneus): There are two Eurynome's that feature prominently in Greek mythology, and some believe that the first one was a member of the original primordial Titans, along with her husband, Ophioneus. Together they fought against Kronos and Rhea in a battle to rule and were ultimately defeated. There is much less written about Ophion and the first Eruynome, but they are held to be the equivalent of Kronos and Rhea, and would therefore be either siblings or somehow placed before them within the line of primordial gods.

The other Eurynome was a daughter of the Titans Oceanus and Tethys and was also the third wife of Zeus (see Chapter 5: Zeus and His Lovers), to whom she bore the three Charities (Three Graces).

The Uranides

Of Uranus; (the word origin of the element Uranium is Uranus).

The first Titans ruled from Mount Othrys and were 6 males, Kronos, Iapetus, Hyperion, Oceanus, Coeus, Creus, and 6 females, Theia, Rhea, Mnemosyne, Phoebe, Tethys, and Themis. When Uranus banished his first children, the Hekatonkheires and the Cyclopes, Gaia implored her Titans to free them, so they set themselves as sentinels around the earth to capture Uranus as he descended to earth.

"When Ouranos descended down to Gaia, the youngest of her sons, Kronos the Titan, attacked with the blade fashioned of flint by Gaia herself, castrating him and hurling his genitals into the deep waters from which came the blood that produced the foot soldiers, vengeance and the honey tree; also emerged Aphrodite Ourania."

The mention of *foot soldiers* is a reference to the Gigantes, who were not necessarily as large as their name might imply, but were heavily armored and ready for battle. The Erinyes were *vengeance,* the Furies; they embodied all the curses of mankind and reprisal for deceit and animosity. The *honey tree* or ash tree is thought to be the three Meliae or the softer side of the three Fates.

Here we see the beginning of Gaia differentiating herself from Uranus, setting herself as the defiant and protective mother who will defend her children at all cost. Later we will see her rebel again when her son Kronos again imprisons her children, the Cyclopes. This time she turns to Zeus to overthrow his father, Kronos. Ultimately, she will come in conflict with Zeus, who also sends her Titan sons to Tartaros.

If we remember that the gods were seen as the embodiment of the element they represented, it can be interpreted that the stories of Tartaros or what's referred to as the Underworld, may also be interpreted as the womb of Gaia. So her children were literally trapped inside her by her husband Uranus. The Titans give us our first real insight into the world view of the Ancient Greeks. This pantheon represents that society's ideas about heaven and earth, war and peace, agriculture and relationships, and home and family.

Kronos (Cronus): Kronos is the Titan father of Zeus, and should not be confused with Chronos, the God of Time or Father Time. Kronos was allegedly the strongest and the bravest of the Titans and led the attack on his father, Uranus. He was charged by Gaia with saving his brothers, the Cyclopes and the Hekatonkhieres, from the pit of Tartaros. Succeeding in this task, Cronus (Kronos) gained in power and to the great dismay of Gaia, eventually threw them once again back into the earth.

The oracle prophesied that he would be overthrown by one of his children in the same way he had overthrown his own father. Now he grew afraid and decided to swallow them as they were born. One by one, he devoured the first five children of his consort sister Rhea, but she managed to save her baby son, Zeus by hiding him in a cave on the island of Crete.

When Kronos learned of this trickery, he went after Zeus, who was now a strong young man. Instead, Zeus disguised himself as a servant and served up a strong poison. Cronus drank it and vomited up the stone which was fed to him by Rhea in place of the baby Zeus, and he spit out the other five children of Rhea, who rose against him in a battle to rule the universe.

Iapetus: The God of Craftsmanship and the father of the four Iapetionides: Atlas, Prometheus, Epimetheus, and Menoetius. The Greeks believed that the earth was held apart from the heavens by four pillars. Iapetus was the personification of the pillar of the West, the other three being represented by his brothers Creus, Coeus, and Hyperion. Together, they were believed to have guarded the four corners of the earth waiting for their father, Uranus, to come to earth, where Kronos would finally castrate him at the bequest of Gaia.

Hyperion: The God of Wisdom and Watchfulness and father of Helios the Sun, Selene the Moon, and Eos the Dawn. He was the pillar of the East.

Oceanus (Okeanos): The God of the Rivers and all aqueous elements of nature; he and his wife-sister Tethys did not participate in the war with the Olympians and therefore were not later banished to Tartaros with the other Titans.

Coeus (Koios): The God of Intellect; he was the pillar of the North and father to Asteria and Leto, who would become one of Zeus' lovers.

Creus (Krios): The God of the Winds and the pillar of the South.

Theia: The Goddess of Light who gave brilliance to the gems of the earth.

Rhea: The Guardian Mother; with her brother Cronus, she gave birth to six children who would later be known as the Immortal

Olympians – Hestia, Hades, Demeter, Poseidon, Hera, and Zeus.

Mnemosyne: The first of the Titans and the Goddess of Memory; she was the mother of the nine Muses, whose father was Zeus. It was believed that the Muses gave the gifts of extraordinary speech to the kings and poets of men.

Phoebe: The Goddess of Prophecy; she was associated with the Oracle of Delphi; with her brother Coeus she bore Asteria and then Leto, who was the mother of the twin Olympians, Apollo and Artemis. Later in the war between the Titans and the Olympians, in which she refused to participate and in which the Titans were defeated, she was spared being banished to Tartaros.

Tethys: The Goddess of Rivers who, with Oceanus, gave birth to the river gods.

Themis: The Goddess of Law and Moral Order; also responsible for the never-ceasing rotation of time. She worked through the three Fates or Moires, who decided the lifetime of each human.

The Iapetionides

Atlas: In some interpretations, Atlas was the giant who held up the earth, and in others he held up the sky or both earth and sky. As a child of Iapetus, he took part in the Titanomachy, the great battle between the Titans and the Olympians, and it was for that act that Zeus gave him the punishment of forever being the pillar that held up the world.

Prometheus: Prometheus is "forethought" and is most notable as the god who gave mankind the gift of fire, a tool that was the protected domain of the gods. For this he was punished by being chained to a rock where an eagle would eat his liver each day, whereupon it would grow back and be eaten again. His fate was eventually changed by Heracles and Chiron, the Centaur.

Epimetheus: This is "afterthought", the brother of Prometheus who, together, were assigned the task of creating man. However, Epimetheus gave all his gifts to the animals instead of man, which is what prompted Prometheus to steal the gift of fire. Prometheus and Epimetheus are also interpreted as being the "representatives" of mankind. Later, Epimetheus would marry Pandora who bore Pyrrha, who married Deucalion, a descendant of Prometheus. Pyrrha and Deucalion are important because they were the only two humans who survived the Great Flood created by Zeus when he discovered that mankind had become irreverent.

Menoetius: This is the God of Insults and Rash Action. He features in the Titanomachy during which he is slain and sent to Tartaros. Later, during Heracles' attempt to capture Cerberus, the dog who guarded the gates of the Underworld (the Twelfth Labor), Menoetius challenged Heracles to a wrestling match and lost.

Chapter 2: Zeus and the Immortal Olympians

When we think of Greek Gods, we think of the Olympians because they have been the most written about and the most popularized of all the gods of antiquity, but the Olympians are actually the Fifth Order of Immortals, not the second or third, a mistake made by many because of the way they appear in the genealogy.

They presided over the universe and had authority over the legions of lesser gods and spirits, an honor gained by winning the Titanomachy. They are not all good and noble, however, and were known to lie, cheat, steal, torment, and terrorize humans often. They also spawned the most heroes, figures humans could relate and aspire to.

In the original marriage of Kronos and Rhea, both Titans, there were 6 siblings, three boys and three girls.

The battle between the Titans and the Olympians, known as the Titanomachy, lasted ten years and was fought long before the birth of man. Sometimes referred to as the First Olympian War (with the Gigantomachy being the second), it was a great battle for rule of the universe, one which ended in the defeat of the Titans and which proved the younger Olympian Gods to be superior. When the battle ended, the three brothers drew lots to see who would rule each portion of the universe.

"So through their blood ties did Hades, with Zeus and Poseidon his brothers, release the mighty Cyclopes and Hekatonkeires from Tartaros to forge weapons and armor to battle the Titans. From exile they came and grateful for their release, they made the helmet for Hades that he might become the invisible one; the unseen among the gods, and for Zeus a thunderbolt, for Poseidon a three-pronged spear.

"Long days did the offspring of Rhea pass in battle against all the mighty forces of Kronos, who fought for his throne against the prophecy, and against the Four Pillars: Iapetus who was the West, Creus the North who was the Wind, Coeus the South, and Hyperion the East. Even the Guardian Mother [Rhea] battled against her own who would rule over the Titan Gods, and in the end, all save Phoebe, Okeanos and Tethys were banished to Tartaros for all eternity, for gods cannot die."

In Ancient Greek mythology, the Twelve Olympians are most commonly considered to be Zeus, Poseidon, Hestia, Hera, Demeter, Athena, Apollo, Artemis, Ares, Aphrodite, Hephaestus, and Hermes. Some include Dionysus. Although Hades was one of the original six siblings from Rhea and Kronos, he did not reside on and never visited Mount Olympus and is therefore not referred to as an Olympian God. Others, such as Poseidon who lived under the sea, were free to visit Olympus at any time.

Hades: God of the Underworld and Wealth, Ruler of the Dead, whose domain is referred to as Tartaros, the belly of the earth, and metaphorically, the womb of Ge (Gaia).

"He bore down upon Kronos, fighting ferociously, proving himself a valiant warrior, and so it was that he would rule the sleeping and the dead in the place of punishment, yet his responsibility was large, for the spirits of those who sleep and dream, who die or are banished from the earth must be diligently cared for.

"And in his duties he grew lonely and took Persephone as a wife, but she was brightness and detested the things of darkness. So he [Hades] bargained with his brother Zeus and his sister, Demeter, the mother of Persephone, that the bride would live in Tartarus one month for each seed she ate."

Poseidon: God of the Sea who could strike up tempests and towering waves, or ride his golden chariot over the waves to quiet them. He could strike the ground with his trident and cause the earth to quake and split. His wife was

Amphitrite the sea nymph who bore him Triton, a son.

"The Lord of the Seas gathered rain and clouds and shook the earth from under the waters, for he was quick to take offense, and in this, he punished Odysseus eight years. Though other sailors were kept safe at sea by the mighty god, he exacted his retribution against Odysseus with storms and swells, monsters and horrifying sirens who could hypnotize a man and render him helpless to resist their call, thus causing them to jump into the sea and drown."

Zeus: God of the Heavens and ruler of Mount Olympus; King of the Gods and God of Thunder and Lightning. At least one scholar, Pherekydes of Syros, believed that Zeus has always existed as Zas, one of the primordial deities, along with Chronos (Father Time) and Chthonie, the prototype figure of Gaia.

"Now the Titans were dismantled and sent to Hades, and the Olympian Age was begun. Zeus of the Thunderbolt ruled Olympus and all the other gods, but the new Lord of the Sky was a jealous and vengeful god, and his fearsome bolts brought thunder and scorching fire to the land. He was abusive in his powers and rained his thunderbolts at any who displeased him.

"But the Olympians grew tired of his undisciplined power and sought to dethrone him. They sent him to Hades by trickery, and so it was that his son, Perseus, came to relieve him from his torture.

"Perseus engaged the wisdom and knowledge of Hephaestus who was the Smith, creator of the Gates which locked the entrance to the Underworld. For he had been to the cave of the Gorgon, Medusa, and had killed the mighty monster of Poseidon and broke the chains that held Andromeda. His feats were great, but none would demand more courage and wit than gaining the gates of Hades.

"One hundred doors did confound the enterer and all but one would kill. But Haphaestus' maze was made with magical walls which moved and changed; they caused Perseus to slide along the smooth stone into the pit and the walls raised all around him. The labyrinth seemed to live of its own accord, the great stone walls rising and falling, creating new tunnels where there were none until the doorway to Tartaros was revealed and the Hound of Hell reared its many heads.

"So once saved, he [Zeus] became a more benevolent ruler who managed to contract a way out for those who would repent of their disrespect of the God of Thunder. And so it was that Heracles and Chiron were able to relieve poor Prometheus from his agony, who had edified man with the gift of fire and was bound in chains to be eaten by an eagle."

The three sisters were:

Hestia (Vesta): Goddess of the Hearth and Home. She is said to be the only chaste god.

"But Vesta [Hestia] among them all was sought by Poseidon, the great God of the Sea, for she was lovely to behold, and Apollon sought her for a wife. In her unwillingness to be thusly wed, she enlisted the shield of Zeus and Athena to protect her and touching the aegis, swore an oath that she would remain a maiden. And he [Zeus] honored her, so that all the temples of the gods should do likewise, and among mortal men she would be chief among the goddesses, so bound that even Aphrodite cannot contest. Her place shall be in the midst of the house and she shall receive the richest portion."

Hera: Goddess of Marriage and Protector of Women; wife and sister of Zeus, whom she tormented relentlessly for his unfaithfulness, along with his lovers.

"...so when the Gods of Olympus grew tired of Zeus and the abuses he made of his power, they plotted against him, spurred by Hera, his wife, and in doing so, they bound him up. But Briareus alone, a son of Uranus and Gaia, unbound him in the lull and he [Zeus] pulled from his vest the thunderbolt, striking the rebels down. To Hera, he hung her from the sky on chains made of gold, fashioned with the Smith's magic from which she may not be unleashed, until she wept and Zeus felt for her. Thus he drew from her an oath, that she would ever after be loyal to him.

"But Hera's wrath, though contractually bound, needed a mark, and so it was to fair Alcmene of the line of Perseus she turned her venomous glare and to her infant, Heracles, spawned from the lust of Zeus. For Zeus had transpired to change events to favor his arrival upon the girl and disguised as her husband, Amphitryon, he lay with her for three nights. And when Amphitryon returned from his battles, he too lay with her and in her womb now were two babes, Heracles and Iphicles.

"And the Goddess Hera was jealous and called upon Lucina to bind her hands and feet so the child could not come forth, but a handmaiden of Alcmene tricked the goddess and so it was that Heracles was born."

Demeter: Goddess of the Harvest, whom Zeus seduced, and to whom she bore Persephone.

"All the gods were in attendance to the wedding of Kadmos [Cadmus] and Harmonia, yet two did lie in the field, with thrice plowed furrows for the fertility rites of spring. And Iasion, a prince of Samothrake, lusted for Demeter the goddess, and she loved his beauty, so she lured him into the field where, in the rich soil, he inspired her loins to produce her offspring.

"Yet Zeus knew of their conjoining and smote him and killed him with his thunderbolt for his insolence that he should lie with Demeter, whom Zeus had also loved."

The Palace of Mount Olympus

The Titanomachy (see Chapter 8: The Battles) was fought and won from Mount Olympus by the original six sons and daughters of the Titans Rhea and Kronos, and this would become the place from which they would rule. It was said to have been the highest mountain in Greece, considered to be the center of the world, a place filled with brilliant light and warmth, and a place where mortals could not go.

Aphrodite: The Goddess of Love, Beauty, Eternal Youth, and Fertility who rose from the foam of the sea; wife of Hephaestus (son of Zeus and Hera); mother of Eros (God of Love) by Ares (God of War).

Apollo: God of Light, Music and Poetry; God of Healing; he is closely associated with the Muses; twin brother to Artemis; son of Zeus and Leto, who was a Titan.

Ares: God of War; he was the curse of mortals; he was always accompanied by Conflict, Strife, Terror, Trembling, and Panic; violence and bloodshed followed him wherever he went; son of Zeus and Hera.

Artemis: Goddess of Hunting and Unmarried Girls; twin sister to Apollo; daughter of Zeus and Leto.

Athena: Goddess of Wisdom; Goddess of Arts and Crafts; Protector of Heroes in Battle; said to be the favorite daughter of Zeus, she sprung from his head fully grown and fully armed, wearing a helmet and robe.

Dionysus: God of Wine; youngest son of Zeus by Semele, a mortal, who was tricked by Zeus and then consumed by his presence in God form.

Hephaestus: God of Fire; God of Craftsmen and Protector of Blacksmiths, Goldsmiths and Carpenters; son of Zeus and Hera; husband of Aphrodite.

Hermes: God of Shepherds, Merchants, Travelers, and Thieves; Guider of the Souls of the Dead to the underworld; Zeus' son and personal messenger by Maia, a nymph; father of Pan.

The generations of gods bore hundreds of children both mortal and immortal, and some figure more prominently than others.

Asclepius: The son of Apollo and a mortal princess, Coronis who died in childbirth. The child was raised by Chiron (Kheiron) the Centaur who taught him the art of healing and the use of medicine and he grew up having revealed his gift of restoring the dead to life. For this, Zeus destroyed him, for no one was to go against the Fates.

Charites: The three Graces were Aglaia (Splendor), Thalia (Rejoicing), Euphrosyne (Festivity), the daughters of Zeus and Eurynome, though some say they were the daughters of Helios and Aegle, a naiad (water nymph).

Dioscuri: Castor and Pollux (Polydeuces), the twin sons of Leda, daughter of King Thestius, and Zeus.

Eileithyia (Ilithyia): Goddess of Childbirth, daughter of Zeus and Hera.

Eros: God of Love

Hebe: Cupbearer to Zeus before Ganymede.

Heracles: The great grandson of Perseus of the line of Zeus; he was the only man born of a mortal woman who became a deity after his death.

Horae: These were the Goddesses of the Seasons and the daughters of Zeus and Themis: Auxo (Growth), Eunomia (Order), Pherusa (Substance), Carpo (Fruit), Dice (Justice), Euporia (Abundance), Irene (Peace), Orthosie (Prosperity), Thallo (Green shoots or buds).

Leto: Daughter of the Titans Coeus and Phoebe, one of Zeus' lovers before Hera, mother of Artemis and Apollo.

Nike (Winged Victory): The personification and Goddess of the Ideal Victory in battle and sport; daughter of Styx and Pallas.

Tyche: Daughter of Aphrodite and Hermes, she is the Goddess of Prosperity (for a city, not an individual).

Chapter 3: The Creation of Mankind

This is where the fantastic stories begin; where we meet the heroes and villains and witness the trials and triumphs of both gods and men. Remember that these stories were created before the age of enlightenment, industrialization, and technology. They came before the development of science as we know it and man's exploration of his universe, so everything was left up to the imagination, and the imagination was based solely on what the Ancient Greeks saw as their world.

Prometheus and the Gift of Fire

Prometheus was charged by Zeus with the creation of mankind, along with his brother Epimetheus, both descendants of the Titan Iapetus and therefore Titans themselves. Their mother was Clymene, an Oceanid born of Oceanus and Tethys, both Titans.

Prometheus was the God of Forethought and he began to mold man out of clay, mixing the earth with the waters from the sea. He gave man two legs to stand on so he would be nobler than the other beasts of earth, able to look up at the heavens and not be resigned to looking down at the earth as the other animals did. He made man in his own image; the image of the gods.

Prometheus was a kind and thoughtful god who loved his creations and showed them favor whenever he could. In his obsession to edify them and give them an advantage over the rest of Nature, he wanted to give them a special gift.

His brother, Epimetheus, was the God of Afterthought. He saw fit to give his gifts to the animals, giving each one a means of defense against the elements and a means to hunt for food. He gave each of the animals a different gift - claws and wings, horns and speed, each one suitable to their individual nature.

But when he told Prometheus he had given all his gifts to the animals and had none left to give to man, Prometheus became angry.

What could he give to man to set him apart and help him survive?

He would give him the gift of fire! It would keep him warm, cook his food and allow him to forge weapons. It would protect him from predators and give him light in the darkness. But fire was the domain of the higher gods and therefore was unavailable for even Prometheus to give away to man as he saw fit, so he enlisted the help of the goddess Athena. She gave him entrance to the heavens and guided him to the blazing chariot of the sun, where he lighted a torch and returned to earth to give his precious gift to man.

Zeus was enraged when he learned of Prometheus' deception. He feared that man would become too powerful, even more powerful than the gods, so he punished Prometheus by chaining him to a rock high in the Caucasus Mountains. Day after day, he would have his liver eaten by a vulture. Each day the liver would grow back and the vulture would come again and eat it. The punishment was meant to be perpetual, but as you will see, Heracles had a hand in eventually setting him free with the help of the Centaur, Chiron.

Pandora's Jar

Zeus had punished Prometheus for stealing fire from the gods, but he also punished man for accepting the gift, though he was innocent of the deception behind that gift. Zeus' revenge was subtle and everlasting.

Woman had not yet been created, so he gave an order to one of his sons, Hephaestus, to create the first woman, fashioned after a beautiful goddess. When the Four Winds breathed life into her clay body, she was attributed with a gift from each of the gods and goddesses to make her very appealing to man. She received beauty, a talent for music and poetry, persuasion and kindness, skill with the bow and craftsmanship, among other gifts. She was adorned with precious robes and jewels and named Pandora, which means "the gift of everything".

When it came time for Zeus to bestow his gift upon Pandora, he gave her the gift of curiosity along with a sealed jar and a warning not to open it. He set Pandora on the earth with Hermes to guide her and bring her to Epimetheus as a gift from Zeus.

Of course Epimetheus, who was rash and careless in thought, was immediately taken with her, but Prometheus warned him not to accept gifts from Zeus, who would surely trick him. Soon, however, the two were married and living happily, but Pandora was ever-curious about the jar she was given by Zeus, until finally she could not restrain herself. She removed the lid and out sprang the evils that would plague mankind to the end of his days – disease, envy, spite, revenge, anxiety and misfortune.

But Zeus was not without his kindness. He had also put hope into the jar and it flew out into the world of men along with the evils. So no matter how many evils befall a man, hope will be by his side to help him endure.

In this story, we see justification for all of man's shortcomings, and the plagues of mankind might be the original *vengeance* handed down from the wrath of Ouranos after his castration. Although Zeus is the perpetrator in this case, each succession of gods seems to have a similar agenda both for man and for each other, with shortcomings of their own and just enough beneficence to make them ultimately loveable.

Here, innocent man takes the fire of the gods, a power that might him "equal or greater than the gods themselves". This is much the same story of the creation of Adam and Eve in the Garden of Eden – man seizing the knowledge of good and evil, a power that would eventually see him growing stronger in his own right and away from the control of a god. The story of Prometheus creating man from dust or clay in the image of the gods, filling the empty vessel with the breath of life, then Pandora's Jar which parallels man's fall at the hands of the curious nature of woman, is essentially the same story told in the Old Testament.

The Fates (Moirae) and Spirits: The Second Class of Immortals

It's a good idea at this point to take a brief step back to gain some understanding of how the Spirits played into man's reality at that time. The Spirits are considered the Second Class of Immortals.

The Ancient Greeks believed that everything about their lives was under the control of the gods, and included in that control was life itself; that the divinities gave each individual an allotted time on earth. Everything about the future was fixed in place at birth and not subject to change, though as you will see, the gods seem to intervene often to change the fate of a man, often with great consequences.

The Fates or Moirae governed the threads of life and the portions to which they decided he would be entitled. The Goddesses of Fate personified the mortality of mankind. Klotho (Clotho) was the Spinner of the Threads of Life. Lakhesis was the Apportioner who measured out how much thread each individual would receive at birth. Atropos, the Cutter, had the duty of cutting the thread when the time came, an act which could not be changed or turned. The existence of the Fates and their legends solidifies our modern belief that we die "when it's our time" or "when our time comes".

Some believe that the Fates are the daughters of Zeus, but it's more likely they are the children of Gaia or Rhea unless we hold to the theory that Zas or Zeus existed from Chaos, and even the vengeful Hera had reason to fear them, for even gods were bound to their decisions regarding the fates of men. This is why the Oracle at Delphi was so well-respected. Oracles were the soothsayers, the ministers who told an individual, when asked, what the Fates had in store for them.

The Fates were not unkind and would sometimes allow changes to be made in the lives of those who pleaded, but these changes almost always came at great cost, and though the path might be changed, with few exceptions, the end never was.

In addition to determining the length of a person's life, they followed a person's steps, and directed the consequences of his actions which were in strict accordance with the counsel of the gods, particularly Zeus, to whom they were accountable. But as you have already seen, Zeus was not completely without kindness either. If he chose to do so, he could save a person from their fate, even at the final hour.

The Fates, however, could not interfere in human affairs, but instead simply acted as intermediaries, setting each individual on his course. They determined his allotment, but man was free to do with that as he would. So life was conditional to a point, and each individual could influence how he chose to exercise his gifts and his time on earth.

Also under the instruction of the Fates were the Erinyes, who doled out the punishments for evil deeds.

"So in their great bag, they placed the tokens and drew, each according to their desire, while the great King of the Gods looked on, for he was wont to show favor to his mortal son, who would be the son of sorrow and ambition.

"The Fates were foretold of things to come, both the future and the past, and so they might devise to conform to the divine plan of Zeus, yet they might follow their own whim and add to the fate of Heracles much that should be allotted to another. And so the number was drawn and the deity, who had the power to reveal his favor, did create the true prophesy and Heracles was bound to his fate.

"The spinner rolled and pulled and pedaled and twisted, for the thread should not be broken. His strength was pillared in the twine and his ambition would be the match of his father, Zeus. Yet his sorrows would be the consequence of these gifts and he would be made to choose, one over the other.

"And Clotho handed over her portion to Lachesis, the Disposer, assigning each man his destiny and leaving the thread to unwind according to his will; the path would be uncertain, but the end would not be turned, for Atropos, who carried the abhorred shears, would cut the thread at the apportioned length for a man's time on Earth."

We understand that in this, we are given a certain amount of time on this earth, the allotment of which cannot be changed, but the theme of free will – our choices in the direction our path will take and what we will do with our 'tokens' – is evident and shows the ancient philosophical understanding of life and death in much the same way as many of the world's great religions.

"The runes were thrown and thusly Heracles' fate was drawn. The lots were spun and knotted together, the fibers bent and the length cut for his share, yet mighty Zeus would wield his power to the end of Heracles' days and he would make of his son a star in the heavens for all to remember his great deeds."

The timeline of the Fates set for each man was independent from the rule of the gods, who were bound to the timelines set, with the exception of Zeus, who could use his mercy like a wild card to intercept the final act of The Cutter before it was done, but the gods did not know ahead of time what the Fates had determined, so they were often powerless to change it.

The Second Class of Immortals also included spirits who nurtured life in the four elements, nature goddesses and those that presided over natural phenomena such as springs, clouds, caverns, plants and animals. They inhabited and were responsible for the care of these things, unlike the gods and goddesses who were the personification of these things. Though they were immortal, the spirits were not gods, though they are often the attendants of more important deities.

The Third Class of Immortals are the lesser spirits, the spirits that affected the body and mind. They included Hypnos (sleep), Eros (love), Euphrosyne (joy), Eris (hate), Phobos (fear), Thanatos (death), and Geras (old age).

The Fourth Class of Immortals included gods who controlled the forces of nature and the arts, always at the direction of the god or goddess who personified that element. Into this category fall the Nine Muses and all the Nymphs. (See Appendix II: Orders of Nymphs).

The Nine Muses

There were several daughters of the Titan Goddess Mnemosyne who were fathered by Zeus and who dwelled in the canyons and gorges of Mount Olympus. Each of these daughters had a special gift. They were the personification of knowledge and the arts, particularly literature, dance and music. The new race of men were proving to be hearty and kind and Zeus wanted them to thrive, so he bade his daughters to be a source of inspiration and guide them using their gifts.

But the Muses at times could also be vain and arrogant. They often resented mortals, particularly those favored by the gods, and if any should question the supremacy of the Muses, they would be tricked and tried, sorted and punished. The powers of the Muses were many and if they saw fit to bless a mortal, that person would be great in the use of words, songs, poems, speech and writing, dance, literature and bringing comfort to others with their words.

Writers disagree concerning the number of the Muses. Some say there were only three, and others say there were nine, but the number nine has prevailed. It's likely that the early writings were based on Zeus's early life, and later, as he had more children, the Muses became nine in number.

Another explanation for the discrepancy may be the difference between the primordial muses and the ancient muses. Three ancient Muses are described as being born of Gaia and Uranus, the first being born from the movement of water whose name was Melete (practice), the second who makes sound by striking the air, called Mneme (memory), and a third, who is embodied only in the human voice, is named Aoide (song).

The nine later muses born of Mnemosyne by Zeus were:

Calliope: Muse of Epic Poetry.

Clio: Muse of History, Flutes and Lyric Poetry.

Euterpe: Muse Music and Melancholic Poetry.

Erato: Muse of Odes.

Melpomene: Muse of Tragedy (drama).

Polyhymnia: Muse of Sacred Hymns.

Terpsichore: Muse of Dance.

Thalia: Muse of Comedy and Pastoral Poetry.

Urania: Muse of Astronomy.

It might interest you to know that many of our modern words stem from the word *muse*: Music (meaning *of the muse*), Museum (*hall of the muses* or a place where the muses were worshipped), for example.

To clarify further, the Muses were both the embodiments and the sponsors of performed metrical speech just like the gods were the personification of their individual domains. *Mousike* (music) and poetry were just some of the arts of the Muses. They inspired the arts of Science, Geography, Mathematics, Philosophy, and especially Fine Art and Drama, essentially all areas of learning which was handed down through generations.

Seers, Oracles and Prophets

A person who could "see" the future was said to be an oracle, one who is favored by the gods with the gift of prophesy. These people were known as seers or prophets. They were often priests and even poor mortals who were deemed worthy of such favors because they were wise and had the gift of discernment. But there were also temples and shrines that were referred to as oracles, and the "oracle" could refer to the person and the actual message that was delivered.

Messages given by oracles were designed to be intentionally vague. In this way, there was always room for interpretation and the oracle could never be found wrong. A wrong interpretation was simply chalked up to the fact that the receiver was lacking in faith or the power of understanding.

For example, when the king of Lydia consulted the oracle regarding his intention to attack the armies of Persia, he was told that if he did so, he would put an end to a great kingdom. And so the king proceeded with his plans to attack. However, when his own armies are completely wiped out by the mighty Persians, he utters his dissent to the oracle, who explains that the prophecy was indeed the truth, he just misinterpreted it. A great kingdom was destroyed, it just wasn't the one he thought it would be.

The Oracle of Delphi

This oracle was both a person and a building, probably the most famous of the ancient oracles. It was allegedly located by Zeus when he succeeded in finding the center of the earth, the naval of his grandmother, Gaea, from which all life came.

But the personage known as the oracle is surrounded in mystery. There were people who, when they approached the chasm, began to see the future and behaved erratically, moving in a frenzy, and so the gods deemed that only one person could sit at the chasm. It was to be a woman who would sit on a tripod so as not to fall into the omphalos, and she must be of considerable age and wisdom.

But we're also told that Pytheas, the great Python, was the entity who guarded the omphalos. This would be the personification of the priestess, Phythia. In some stories, Apollo slays the python, and in others, he subdues her and owns her, whereas he then speaks directly through her.

""The great and venerable Phythia raised her head, her body coiled and ready to strike, for she knew that Apollo had come to dethrone her. But Zeus himself had placed her to guard the chasm which was the birthplace of earth, where slept the soul of life and the center of the world; the birthplace of Mother Earth, of Gaea herself, the primordial one.

"This was the Oracle of Gaea, the mother of all. She alone came first from the chasm, born of herself who was the Earth. But Apollo slew the serpent and must now cleanse himself of the deed, for no one, not even the son of Zeus and Leto, the mighty King of the Gods and the daughter of Titans, shall denigrate this sacred ground.

"Eight years he cleansed himself to be made worthy in Zeus' eyes, because the spring at Mount Parnassos was sacred."

In another interpretation, Apollo constrains the serpent and then speaks through her.

"The Prophetai hung their pots over the fire as Pythias sat over the chasm. The sacrificial goat was attended and finally the procession climbed the Sacred Way to the Temple of Apollo. One by one the questions came and from her trance, she delivered to them Apollo's message, but none would understand but the Prophetai, whose rhythmic verse must be discerned, for all obscurity must remain to protect the oracle and test the pilgrim's character."

In a sense, the oracles acted as intermediaries between men and their gods in the same way we might today go to a priest, minister or rabbi to help us understand our path and help us make right decisions. In fact, some 2000 years after most of the writings, during the dark medieval days when no one could talk to the gods except through the high priest who doled out repentance duties as though he were the Zeus himself, man still continued to believe he was powerless to change his fate; that his lot in life was set before birth.

Chapter 4: Zeus v Mankind

Many of the creation stories of old Greece are similar to the creation stories that appear in the ancient texts of religions around the world, but none are so fancifully told as those of the gods and goddess of Ancient Greece.

The Great Flood

Many years had passed since Zeus dealt his punishment to Prometheus and mankind through Pandora and her curious jar of evils. The plagues had been set loose on the world and Zeus decided he would disguise himself as a mortal and travel the earth. He could see the world below Olympus, but he wanted to witness firsthand how mortals were behaving and reacting to his punishment.

What he learned was beyond what he imagined, for man had become all the things he let loose on them. They were evil and wicked, deceitful and without reverence for the gods. They had become thieves, stealing from each other, with the greedy becoming wealthy and the meek left with nothing, not even their own harvest. They made weapons and fought bloody wars between themselves and they even fought brother against brother.

So Zeus saw fit to destroy the world of man. He saw no one who deserved to live upon the earth, not one person who was reverent to mother Gaia and none who worshipped the gods.

But how could he destroy mankind without destroying the earth and the heavens at the same time? A fire might destroy everything the gods stood for, so he decided to use floods to drown all living things.

At this time, Deucalion, the son of Prometheus whom Zeus had punished many years earlier, was at his father's side attempting to chase away the vulture that plagued him. But Prometheus, who had the gift of forethought and vision of the future, knew what Zeus had planned and he instructed his son urgently.

"You must leave this place at once. Go home and prepare for a great flood which Zeus will set upon the world to drown all mankind. You must make preparations to survive. Build a vessel large enough to outlast the rising waters and await the time they will recede and life will begin to take root once again. You must gather supplies with haste and set yourself at the ready, for the waters will come swiftly and no man shall survive.

"So under his father's instructions, Deucalion built a wooden ark that would float upon the flooded land, carrying himself and his family, plus herds of sheep and cattle and food to last many months. As Zeus unleashed the Winds and sent rain howling across the land, Deucalion and his wife, Pyrrha, hurried to close up the ark just as the rains poured from the heavens and the rivers began to swell and rush across the land.

"The water continued to rise for many days, swirling and sweeping away everything in its path until it covered the earth and became one with the sea. For many nights, the ark was tossed until at last the winds and rain stopped and the water began to slowly draw back. The ark was cast upon Mount Parnassus where it lodged, and Deucalion and Pyrrha opened the doors to a desolate place, void of all life.

"They feared they were the only people left alive, so they went to the temple, which had been ruined by the flood, and thanked Zeus for saving them. He took pity on them, for they had never ceased in their worship of him, and sent a Titan to instruct them. He told them to cover their heads and throw the bones of their ancestors over their shoulders. Horrified by the request to do such a disrespectful thing, they obeyed, realizing that they simply had to throw stones, which are the bones of the earth, and out of Mother Earth would spring new life. And so it did. It was a new race as strong as stone, fit to carry on the task of rebuilding the earth after the great flood."

Chapter 5: Zeus and His Lovers

Zeus was king of the Gods of Mount Olympus and reigned over all the lesser gods. He was arrogant and conceited, though not unkind, and had many consorts. It's interesting to note that although the gods were all powerful, they found it necessary to trick each other at times, as you will see in many of the stories.

Metis, the First Wife

Metis was the first wife of Zeus. She was the Titan Goddess of Wisdom and Deep Thought, which is often interpreted as Wise Council. She was an Oceanid born of Oceanus and his sister Tethys. It's been told that she was the first of Zeus' great loves.

Metis was originally the counselor who gave Zeus the poison he was to administer to his father, Kronos, in order to have his siblings regurgitated. Upon sleeping with Metis, however, Zeus became worried because the prophecy stated that she would bear children more powerful than himself who would eventually overthrow him. So he tricked her into becoming a fly, eating her at once and therefore thinking he had forestalled the prophecy. But he did not do so in time. She had already conceived Athena, whose responsibility was now Zeus' to bear, and who would spring from his head fully armed and armored.

To get a better understanding of this rather simplistic representation, here's an excerpt from Hesiod's *Theogony*:

"When she was about to bear gray-eyed Athena, then through the schemes of Gaia and starry Ouranos, he deceived the mind of Metis with guile and coaxing words, and lodged her in his belly."

It was fated that Metis would bear keen-minded children, Athena, Tritogeneia, whose strength would match her father's, and Achilles by the mortal, Paleus, a son who would be high-mettled and resilient, with courage and fortitude; destined to rule over gods and men.

Themis

Next he married Themis, Titan Goddess of Tradition, whose children were the three Hours (Horai), the three Fates (Moirai), and the four Seasons.

"And so it was that Mother Earth and Father Sky united to bring the Titan Themis, who took the oracular seat of her mother and would be the bride of Zeus, bearer of the Seasons [Horai] and the Fates [Morai] that she should be the counselor to the king and the establisher of natural law and order."

Oddly, we're told by another ancient scholar that her children, the Fates "in their golden chariot" brought Themis to the springs of Okeanos, the sacred stair of Olympus, on her wedding day, where she would wed and bear the seasons.

Eurynome

There is more than one Eurynome in Greek mythology and this is likely the same one who, with Ophion, contested against Kronos and Rhea. This one is a Titan elder ocean nymph, daughter of Oceanus and the third wife of Zeus, who bore him the three Graces.

"She bore him three fair-cheeked Kharites (charities), and there in the sanctuary, the holy spot of old, grow cypress trees from the ground in Phigalia where stands a temple in her name, and golden chains bind the wooden image of the sea goddess who lives in the depths of the sea."

Mnemosyne

Mnemosyne, a Titan, was thought to be one of the three elder Titan muses and was the fourth wife of Zeus and whose children were the nine Muses.

"...and she who was the cause of all memory, to give down the stories contained in the minds of the gods, that men might learn the heart of their patron, the one of poets and songs.

And so the tradition might be preserved, each to his next generation, the Goddess Mnemosyne did grant them these gifts, in her daughters, inspiration from the gods, those beautiful epic tales of glory which otherwise are unfathomable to man."

Demeter

Demeter was a sister of Zeus and against her will, he took the form of a bull and gave her Persephone, who would later become part time Queen of the Underworld in a bargain made between Zeus, Hades and Demeter.

"The virgin was swiftly taken by the minion of Hades, down into the pit of Tartaros, the place of loss and grief. The goddess searched endlessly across all the land for her bright child, but the God of the Underworld hid her in the bowels of the pit.

"A dark winter fell across the earth and all things that grew from it were ended. The earth lay barren, so he [Zeus] sent word by Hermes to release the girl to save the earth, but the Lord of the Underworld did give her pomegranate seeds to ease her hunger, and for each seed she ate, a bargain was made that she would spend her time with him.

"And so it was that the flowers returned in spring, for young Persephone ascended above the ground and returned to her mother and they rejoiced, with the sun shining on her brilliant hair."

Persephone had eaten four pomegranate seeds and was bound by the bargain to stay with Hades four months of the year and with Demeter the remainder of the year.

Leto

Leto, mother of the twin gods Apollo and Artemis, was Zeus' lover before his marriage to Hera. She was the Goddess of Motherhood, Modesty and Womanly Demure. In some writings, she is also the Goddess of Night or Goddess of the Light of Day.

"But Leto alone stays by the side of Zeus who delights in thunder; and then she unstrings his bow and closes his quiver and takes his archery from his strong shoulders in her hands and hangs them on a golden peg against a pillar of his father's house. Then she leads him to a seat and makes him sit: and the Father gives him nektar in a golden cup welcoming his dear son... and queenly Leto rejoices because she bare a mighty son and an archer." (Homeric Hymn 3 C7th to 4th BC)

Hera

Hera was to become Zeus permanent wife. She was the patron of marriage and childbirth, having a special interest in protecting married women. Zeus tried several times to court her, but after many unsuccessful attempts, he resorted to trickery, as these gods and goddesses were known to do. He took the form of a rumpled cuckoo, a bird which had the habit of laying its eggs in the nests of other birds. You might appreciate the irony of this when taken in the context of Zeus and his habit of lying with many women, both mortal and immortal.

Hera showed kindness to the bird and took it in, but Zeus's cunning overwhelmed her when he resumed his form and took advantage of her. In this way, Hera was forced to marry him and the union that followed was often fraught with turbulence and jealousy.

When Hera had had enough of Zeus' philandering, she enlisted the help of the other Olympians, most of whom he had treated harshly, and they agreed to let Hera drug him so they could bind him. When Briareus heard of this (he was one of the Hekatonkhieres saved by Zeus), he freed Zeus who then sprang up, grabbed his thunderbolt and raged over the other gods.

Hera was bound in gold chains and dangled from the sky, where she cried all night from the torment. In the morning, Zeus, who had been kept awake by the crying, released her on the condition that she would never again rebel against him. Of course she agreed, but she continued to plague him with jealousy, interfering with his love quests and constant infidelity. She succeeded quite often at surprising him and getting revenge on the innocent mortals who came into his path.

Semele and Her Deadly Wish

Semele, also called Thyone, was a mortal woman, the daughter of Cadmus and Harmonia of Thebes who was tricked by Zeus and then consumed by his presence in God form. She would become the mother of Dionysus, also called Bacchus, by Zeus.

As was his custom, Zeus easily fell in love with other women, and the beautiful Semele was no exception. He was so taken by her that he agreed to grant her anything she wished for. His visits to Semele caused no end of rage in Hera, his goddess wife, so she decided to disguise herself as an old nurse and visit Semele in order to deceive her.

She convinced Semele that it would be wise to ask Zeus to visit her in all of his godly glory and splendor, knowing full well that any mortal who laid eyes upon a god would perish. When Semele put forth her request, Zeus knew he must grant her wish for he had already promised her he would do so, but his heart was heavy for he knew the consequences of this wish. When he appeared in all of his glory, his fire bolts would destroy her.

And so she died, but not before Zeus was able to save their unborn child, whom he called Dionysus. He pulled the infant from her womb and planted it in his thigh to keep it until it was ready to be born. Some say that when Dionysus was fully grown, he went to Tartaros and brought Semele back, and some believe she then was granted the gift of immortality.

Io, the White Cow

Zeus often fell in love with beautiful women on earth or other lesser goddesses, and because Hera was jealous of these other women, he had to create trickery and disguises to hide his deeds from her.

Io was the daughter of a river god. She was beautiful and soft like the waters with an easy spirit, and Zeus could not resist her loveliness. In order to visit her, he ordered a dark thick cloud cover to hide them from Mount Olympus so Hera would not see them, but Hera was curious about the unusual clouds forming over the land when the day had been pleasant and sunny.

She knew of Zeus' trickery and went to earth to unravel the mystery behind the clouds, knowing full well that her husband would be behind this unusual weather. When she found him, he was stroking a beautiful white cow, which was Io disguised by Zeus to conceal his lover. She remarked on its magnificence and asked to have it as a gift, knowing that if Zeus refused, he would reveal Io in the cow.

So he gave Hera the cow and she took it to Argus, the monster with one hundred eyes, to keep guard over her for all eternity. When Io's father found her missing, he searched long and hard for his daughter. When he came upon Argus and the cow, she scratched her name in the dirt with her hoof, "IO", and her father knew it was his beloved daughter.

When Zeus saw the reunion of father and daughter, he took pity on them and sent Hermes to kill Argus. This would prove to be most difficult, for even when Argus slept, he kept some of his eyes open. Clever Hermes decided to tell Argus a tale of great length, so that soon the monster was tired of the dreary tale and each of his eyes began to close. Io was freed, but she was still a cow. Hera drew a promise from Zeus never to love her again, and so it was that Io was changed back into a lovely maiden.

Europa and the Cretan Bull

Europa was the sister of Cadmus, father of Semele. When she was a girl, she was gathering flowers with the other girls in a meadow near the sea. They were a fetching group, but Europa was far more winsome than the others.

Zeus fell in love with her immediately and went to earth disguised as a bull among a herd of bulls, but he had distinguished himself with a silver circle in his brow. As he approached the girls, Europa remarked on his magnificent color and gentle nature. He kneeled before her, inviting her to climb onto his back. Europa, who was the daughter of a king and accustomed to magnificent animals, did so without hesitation.

Zeus instantly rose up and carried her out over the brilliant sea, far across the waves where she witnessed a splendid procession of sea gods riding on dolphins led by Poseidon. Still Europa clung to Zeus' horns and begged the bull not to take her from her home and friends.

He declared himself to be Zeus, God of the Sky and told her not to be afraid, for he was in love with her. So together they went to the island of Crete where Zeus showed himself to her as a god. And so it was that Europa became the mother of Minos and Rhadamanthus.

She fared better than Io, for Hera was never aware of her liaison with Zeus.

Selene

Selene was the Goddess of the Moon and a daughter of the Titans, Hyperion and Theia. She bore Zeus two daughters: Ersa and Pandia.

"The lunar crescent of the Moon [Selene] rose each night and visited upon the boy, for Zeus placed him in a cave that she might lie with him in the darkness. Her winged steeds rose upon the air like the horns of a bull and carried her to meet the shepherd prince, for his eternal youth was a gift from the great god Zeus."

This story tells us that Selene fell in love with a young shepherd prince, Endymion, so Zeus gave him eternal youth and immortality and put him into a deep sleep, whereby Selene could lie with him each night.

Danaë

Danaë was the daughter of King Acrisius whose son, as foretold by the Oracle at Delphi, would grow up and kill the king. In an attempt to counter the fate told by the oracle, he had his daughter locked in an underground house made of bronze where no one would see her. Unfortunately, there needed to be a small opening in the roof for air to enter, and through this opening Zeus made his way to Danaë. Their son was Perseus, the hero who would kill Medusa, the Gorgon.

"And though she was hidden under the ground and shielded by bronze, Zeus had fallen in love with the girl and so changed himself into a dazzling spray of golden light and visited upon her in her black chamber. He moved with fluid grace and lighted the cheerless place until she felt his amorous embrace and they coupled, giving life to the soul of Perseus, their child."

Callisto, the Great Bear

Once again Zeus had fallen in love with someone. This time it was a nymph named Callisto who bore him a son, Arcadia. And once again, Hera, upon hearing that Zeus had fathered yet another child by other than herself, took it out on the female, turning Callisto into a bear. As poor Callisto roamed the woods, she saw her son tried to tell him who she was, but she could only growl. Arcas, the boy, being afraid of the great bear approaching him and growling at him, drew his spear to attack it, but Zeus interceded and turned him into a bear as well in order to protect his lover. They were both placed in the northern sky. It's said that Zeus hurled them up by their tails and this is why their tails are so long.

Ganymede, Zeus' Youth

In Greek mythology, it was perfectly acceptable for a man and a youth to have relations. Ganymede was to the gods the loveliest of humans, and when Zeus saw him, he fell in love with him, so he appeared in the form of an eagle and swept the boy to Mount Olympus, making him his cup-bearer or wine-pourer, replacing his own daughter, cup bearer Hebe, after she was married to Heracles.

Dione

Dione is an interesting character because she is thought to be the female version of Zeus – her name is the feminine form of *Dios* (Latin *deus*, god). She's believed to be the mother of Aphrodite by Zeus and has been described as having come before Hera. This fits the belief that she was the Oracle of Dodona (presided over the oracle), but others say she is a daughter of Oceanus and the mother of Dionysus. Still others believe she came as early as the elements, and was the daughter of Gaia and either Ouranos or Aether.

Homer calls her the mother of Aphrodite, but she is often referred to as the Goddess of Love and is therefore identified as Aphrodite, not Aphrodite's mother.

However, there are four Dione's in Greek mythology, one of them being a nymph who was the daughter of Atlas. It's likely that this Dione is either the Oceanid (water nymph) born of the Titans Okeanos and Tethys, or if one subscribes to the primordial theory of Zas (Zeus), then this could very well be the Dione born of Aether.

Nemesis

Nemesis is the Goddess of Revenge or Divine Retribution. She was also responsible for maintaining balance among men, causing sorrow to give equilibrium for too much happiness. She was the punisher of Narcissus for his unfeeling heart toward his suitors.

Some say she is the daughter of Nyx and others believe she is the daughter of Zeus, yet he sought to lie with her against her will.

"She fled across the land and sea taking many forms, always that she might escape him, and then disguising herself as a goose, for she had not a desire for her father, but clever Zeus took the shape of a swan because his lust was great and he consorted with her violently. From the egg came Helene."

This is the same Helen of Trojan War fame who was kidnapped by the Trojans and rescued by Achilles.

Thaleia

Thaleia was one of the Nine Muses, the Muse of Comedy and Bucolic Poetry, a daughter of Zeus and Mnemosyne. So once again we see Zeus trying to consort with one of his own offspring.

"For Thaleia was taught by Apollo himself and so Zeus became beguiled of her, for she had the gift of laughter and pastoral poetry of which he was much taken. And sweet Mnemosyne had instilled great powers to inspire humans in her mousai, so that Zeus thought to bewilder the girl in order to lie with her. For many nights, his spirit surrounded her until she was dizzy as though with much wine, and he gathered her up and entered into her without her consent.

"For many days, the story tellers were without their ethereal lady. Their words were jumbled incoherency, and no works came from their hands until Zeus had his fill and left her from his spell. Then the muse rose enchanted with the child in her belly."

There are many guesses regarding the children of the union between Thaleia and Zeus. Some say she is the mother of the Korybantes, a frenetic group of spirits whom Zeus appointed to guard the infant Dionysus, and this fits with the frenetic nature of their union, however other writers tell us that the Korybantes were the sons of Apollo and Thaleia. There are also other Thalias in Greek mythology with whom Zeus had relations, and this may play into the confusion.

Alkemene

This woman was Zeus's great granddaughter, the wife of Amphitryon, a general of Thebes. She was the daughter of Perseus and Andromeda, best known for being the mother of Heracles by Zeus.

For this liaison, Zeus disguised himself as Amphitryon while the general was off fighting, and consorted with her for three nights during her husband's absence during which time he bragged about his (Amphitryon's) military feats. When her husband returned and began regaling his triumphs, she told him he had done so the night before, and in this way, they learned that Zeus had come to her in disguise.

"And he [Zeus] shouted to all the world, that they should know a child would be born, conceived by him, who would prove to be the greatest in all the land. But Hera had sworn a curse on her and with the help of Lucina, the Goddess of Childbirth, bound her legs and hands that she could not deliver the child. Yet a mistress to Alcamene discerned her trouble that it was of the Goddess Hera, and announced the babe was indeed delivered safely, to which

Lucina reacted without wit, releasing her hands and legs and Heracles jumped from the womb."

Heracles would later be deified, the only human to receive that honor. You will see others born of gods and mortals who were considered gods, but they were not born as humans. Dionysus is an example of this. He was the child of Zeus and Semele, a mortal, but he was born as an immortal, not a human.

Chapter 6: The Classic Myths of Gods and Mortals

The best stories of Greek mythology combine tales about divine beings and how the Greeks understood the world before man's venture into the world of science. But myths are not always fact. Legends, on the other hand, might be based in historical events and many have been retold in classic literature such as the *Iliad*, the *Odyssey* and the *Aeneid*. The stories can be entertaining as well as educational regarding the Ancient Greeks' understanding of nature, war, and societal values, among other things.

Persephone and the Dark Winter of Demeter

Persephone was a daughter of Demeter, one of the Olympian Goddesses and sister of Zeus by Kronus and Rhea, the Titans.

One day the high spirited girl was out in the sunny world at springtime running through the flowers and enjoying Nature. Her mother was Goddess of the Harvest, so she was born loving all things that grew from the earth and spending much of her time with her mother who loved the earth. There they had many happy days together watching things grow and blossom and change with the seasons.

This bright sunny day, Persephone was out picking lilies and violets and it seemed she just could not get her fill. She wandered further and further from her friends until, finally, she could not hear them when they called to her. As she wandered into a meadow, she heard a rumbling noise that seemed as though the rocks were battling with the mountains, and suddenly the earth split open into a cavern before her.

From the cavern came a grim-looking man riding on a brilliant golden chariot pulled by magnificent black horses. He wore black armor and his black hair and beard flew in the wake of his speed.

Persephone began to run from the man for she knew that nothing good could rise from the bowels of the earth, but the man grabbed hold of her and pulled her into the chariot. He directed his horses back into the earth as quickly as he had appeared and the earth closed up behind them.

She cried out to her friends, but alas, they could not hear her. They searched and searched. They saw her basket with its flowers strewn about, but she was nowhere to be found.

The chariot sped on, deeper and deeper through dark tunnels. Hades, the God of the Underworld, had captured her. He claimed to have fallen in love with her with her golden hair and sunny disposition, and would never let her leave!

As they crossed the River Styx, where the souls of the dead crossed over, they approached the entrance to the palace of Hades which was guarded by the monstrous Cerberus, the three-headed dog who fortified the opening.

As they entered the gate to the kingdom, Persephone shivered at the thought of never being able to leave this ghostly place, for she was to become Queens of the Underworld, with a cold throne in a cold palace, and though she was given a gold crown with brilliant jewels to complement her sunny nature, her heart was a cold as ice and she would not eat or drink of any of the offerings at her table.

Demeter alone had heard Persephone's screams as they echoed over the land, over the mountains and across the seas as she was taken by Hades to Tartaros. So she left Olympus and disguised herself as an old woman. She wander the earth searching for her daughter for nine days and nights, calling to the mountains and rivers, the forests and streams. Her heart was heavy and she was deep in grief.

When she at last came upon the very spot where Persephone was abducted, she encountered a man who told her he had heard the thundering noise and had seen the chariot spring from the cavern. He told her how the man in the chariot grabbed the girl as she picked flowers and how the earth had closed up around them.

Demeter grew angry for she knew that no one ever escaped the underworld and no man could enter to rescue her lovely daughter who was now doomed to imprisonment, never again to see the light of the sun or the flowers in springtime.

She took her wrath out upon the earth, rendering it cold and barren. Trees no longer bore fruit, everything withered and sheep and catted died from hunger. It was a cold cruel winter for man. Zeus knew that if Demeter continued in this way, mankind would perish, so he pleaded with Demeter to reverse her curse upon the earth. They made an agreement that he would see to the rescue and release of Persephone and Demeter would replenish the earth, but there was one condition; Persephone must not have eaten any of the food of the dead.

He sent Hermes, his messenger, to the underworld to secure her release. To her surprise, Hades would not go against Zeus' wishes and agreed to let her go. He offered her sustenance for her journey in the form of pomegranate seeds, for she had not eaten in many months, and in this way, he knew that if she ate even one of the seeds, she would be bound by Zeus' agreement to return to him.

She ate four seeds then climbed onto the golden chariot. Hermes took her to the temple of Demeter where she was welcomed, but Demeter questioned her about whether or not she had eaten any of the food of the dead. When she heard the details of the contract with Zeus, she wailed and cried. Zeus took pity on her and decided to make a compromise. She would return to Tartaros for only four months of each year, one month for each seed she had eaten, and that is why each year, when Persephone is with Hades, the earth becomes cold and barren. In springtime, when she returns to her mother, the earth springs forth with new life, grasses and fruits and flowers all following in their natural order.

Athena and the Vanity of Arachne

Athena was the Goddess of Wisdom, daughter of Zeus and Metis who sprang from the head of Zeus fully armed and armored. She was fond of spinning and weaving, and taught this art to women. She thought hers were the most beautiful weavings in all the world.

Arachne was a mortal who thought her weaving was far more beautiful than any in the land, even more beautiful than the weaving of the Goddess Athena. When Athena heard Arachne bragging that her weavings were superior, she descended to earth disguised as an old woman and went to Arachne's hut. There the wood nymphs gazed in wonder at the magnificent intricate patterns Arachne wove from her threads.

The old woman (Athena) warned Arachne not to compete with the goddess and to ask her pardon. But Arachne was vain and boasted even further, saying she was not afraid of the goddess. She even posed a challenge, saying the goddess should come down and engage in a competition to see whose weavings were grander. Suddenly, Athena revealed herself and accepted the challenge.

Arachne was startled and afraid, but did not back down. They set their looms to work using all sorts of threads in brilliant gold and silver and blue and every color in the rainbow. But Athena wove a warning into her cloth; a sign that Arachne had better give up and concede. The vain conceited girl continued to weave the gods and their weaknesses into her pattern.

Athena was outraged. The girl's cloth was fine indeed and this made her even angrier. She would not be outdone by a mortal so she tore Arachne's cloth and placed a spell of shame upon her, which prompted Arachne to hand herself by one of her beautiful threads.

Athena, feeling sorry for the girl, let her live, but only as a spider who would hang by a thread and spin webs for all eternity.

Leto the Titan and the Tears of Niobe

Many mortals met their downfall when they foolishly challenged the gods of Olympus or when they refused to worship them, and Niobe, Queen of Thebes, was one such mortal.

Niobe was the granddaughter of Zeus who fathered Tantalus by a mortal, and she had a loving husband and fourteen children, but her downfall began when she set herself above the Goddess Leto, the Titan.

As it happened, Niobe was at a celebration to honor Leto, the mother of Artemis and Apollo. The temple was filled with worshippers who lit incense and prayed to Leto to show them favor. For reasons unknown, Niobe suddenly saw this as foolish and commanded her people to cease their silly behavior, claiming the she was their queen and they should be bowing and kneeling to her, offering her their gifts, sacrifices and vows of loyalty.

The wrath of Leto was great. Niobe had set herself up as being more important than the goddess because she had twelve children and Leto had only two. So she sent her two children, the twins Apollo and Artemis, to teach Niobe a lesson. The twins set themselves high on a tower in the grand plaza where the sons of Niobe pranced about on their horses. One by one they cast an arrow into them, dropping them lifeless to the ground. One by one, Niobe's sons died.

When she heard the crying and wailing of the people, she ran to the plaza and found her sons, then began to cream with grief. Still, her pride got the better of her and she waved her fist at the sky, yelling to the goddess Leto, for she still had seven children and Leto had only two.

Seven more arrows flew through the air and felled the seven daughters of Niobe. She was so overcome with grief that she couldn't move, and except for the flowing of her tears, she seemed as dead as stone. And so it was that the gods had turned her into a stone figure that is wet with flowing tears to this very day.

Pygmalion's Stone Woman

Pygmalion was a sculptor, a mortal who had many disappointments regarding his relationships with women, so he vowed never to marry. His talent for sculpting was a great gift that kept him busy throughout his life, and to this he devoted himself.

One day, he decided to create a perfect woman, one made from stone, one who could never disappoint him because she would be made from marble. He chiseled and chipped day after day, and a little at a time, the stone began to reveal his work in the form of a woman of great beauty. She seemed to be filled with warmth and a spirit of gentleness, though

Pygmalion knew this was only in his imagination. Yet she seemed genuinely intelligent to him and filled with vivacity.

And so it was that Pygmalion began to envision that this woman of stone was real. He kissed her and held her hand, he talked to her and expected a response. But there was no response from his marble woman. He continued to pretend. He imagined her to be alive; a wife he could love; someone who was real! He dressed her in exquisite robes and adorned her with fine jewels. He gave her gifts of flowers and shining shells and he named her Galatea.

But the day came when Pygmalion could no longer bear the lifelessness of his Galatea and he cried out to her in his misery. The day was a special one, for it was the day of the Festival of Aphrodite, the Goddess of Love. Legend tells us that on this day only, all unhappy lovers who came to the temple and prayed to the goddess would be granted the love they desired in their heart.

Pygmalion prayed to the goddess in the temple, asking that his statue would become a real woman, alive and able to return his love. When he returned home, he was full of hope, and sure enough, the statue was warm with life. He kissed her once again and her lips were soft. She smiled and hugged him back, saying she loved him. And so Pygmalion and Galatea were married with the blessing of Aphrodite, and they lived happily ever after.

The Occultation of Orion

Orion was a son of Poseidon and a mighty hunter. He was gifted by his father with the ability to walk over the surface of the waters without peril. When he fell in love with Merope, the daughter of the King of Chios, he slaughtered all the animals on the island and brought them as a gift to his beloved, but she spurned his offerings so he attempted to take her by violence.

"So the king delivered him of much drink that Orion fell into blindness and was cast out onto the seashore. He being lost by his blindness followed the sound of the hammer of the Cyclops until he came to meet the giant who took pity on him and sent him with one of his men to the place of the Sun, Helios, who would restore his sight by the bright rays of his beam.

"And so Orion continued to hunt with Artemis the Huntress who favored him and would take him for a husband. One day, while he was wading through the sea, Apollo thought to chide her and challenged her to hit the thing that bobbed in the water with her arrow. She aimed her arrow and its swift discharge fatally hit her beloved Orion. The waves took him to shore and the goddess mourned her mistake. So she set him in the stars to honor him, with his girdle, sword, lion's skin, and club. And at that moment, the stars were quenched in the light of the moon and the Pleides were paled."

The Pleides were the daughters of Atlas who were pursued by Orion for seven years. Zeus, upon hearing their plea for help, changed them into doves. In the constellations, Orion is seen behind the Pleides as if immortalizing the chase.

Echo and the Wrath of Hera

Echo was a mountain nymph and a great talker. It seemed that wherever she was and whomever she was with, the conversation always ended with the last words of Echo. She and the other nymphs often hunted in the woods, swam in the mountain streams and gathered berries for meals.

One day, Hera was about spying on the nymphs. She suspected that her husband, Zeus, had been dallying with one of them, and she was determined to catch him in this act of betrayal. Echo thought she would try to protect the other nymphs. She did not know which one was Zeus' favorite, but she engaged Hera in conversation so her friends could escape. Hera was on a mission and did not want to take the time to engage in polite conversation. But Echo was childish and continued to talk while the other nymphs escaped Hera's gaze.

Hera's wrath now became tripled. She was already angry with Zeus for visiting a nymph, now this nymph outsmarted her and let the others get away so she gave her a punishment that seemed fitting. Echo was doomed to never being able to speak first and she was made to always have the last word.

This didn't bother Echo too much because she liked to talk anyway, but when she met and fell in love with the handsome hunter, Narcissus, she tried to talk to him and was unable to do so unless he spoke first. After following him through the woods and trying to gain his attention, he finally noticed her, he called to her to come. All she could do was repeat his words. "Come out from your hiding," he called. "Come out from your hiding," she repeated. She appeared before him and thinking she was some sort of magical creature, bade her stay away. "Stay away," she repeated.

This went on for some time until finally Narcissus fled. Her shame was so great that she went into a cave and lived until the end of her days. The only thing that remains is her voice, which continues to echo through the mountains whenever anyone calls out.

The Vanity of Narcissus

There are several stories behind the youth Narcissus, a son of Kephisos (Cephissus), a river god, and Lariope, a sea nymph regarding his fate. When he was a boy, Lariope was forewarned by a seer that he would live a long and happy life, provided he did not become self-aware. He grew into a beautiful young man who was admired and loved by all who saw him, but they loved him for his beauty and he became cold and heartless, rejecting suitors in a cruel and callous way.

One noteworthy young admirer named Armeinias was bitterly rejected by Narcissus, and he reached out to the Goddess Nemesis, Goddess of Justice. She was a sister to the three Fates. The young nymph asked Nemesis to mete out the same cruel rejection by a lover he showed to others so that he would know the pain he caused. The goddess heard the prayer and devised a particularly suitable punishment for Narcissus, one that would play itself out in a most unusual way.

One day Narcissus happened upon a quiet pool with silvery waters and a calm surface that reflected the heavenly clouds. He kneeled beside it thinking he would take a cool drink, and in the pool he saw a magnificent-looking young man. He believed the image to be a resplendent water spirit and remarked that he had never seen anyone so beautiful.

When he cupped his hands into the water to drink, the image faded and disappeared. When the water stilled itself, the image of the spirit returned. This happened repeatedly until Narcissus fell in love with the image – his own image or reflection. He could not understand why the water spirit continued to flee from him, believing himself to be every bit as handsome as the other.

For many days, he stayed at the pool until he became weak. Each time he tried to leave, the image disappeared and Narcissus could not break himself away to get food and he could not sleep for each time he moved from the pool, the handsome image disappeared.

Finally, Narcissus died and left behind a glorious flower where his body once was. The nymphs gather round the flower and called it Narcissus in his memory.

The ancient Greeks believed that it could be fatal to see your reflection. Mirrored glass had not been invented yet, so it would have been fairly easy to avoid one's own reflection. But if by chance it did happen, their superstition was based in the idea that the spirit or soul would be lost or the person might go insane. This superstition surrounds the idea that they were not to see the inner self which was the domain of the gods who created them.

Narcissus or narcissism was a very popular subject in Freudian psychoanalysis, the term implying an excessive degree of ego-centric behavior generally stemming from emotional immaturity.

Phaëthon and the Chariot of Helios, the Sun God

Phaëthon was a son of Clymene, and Oceanid, and the Sun God Helios. When he was a boy, his mates ridiculed him and did not believe his stories about Helios, his father. As he grew into a young man, he wanted proof, so he asked his mother to give him the truth. She told him to travel far to the east, where he believed the palace of the sun to be.

As he got closer to this place, the light became blindingly bright. He could see the brilliant golden walls of the palace, the glistening rooftop, and the fiery jewels embedded in the doors and lintels, all made of gleaming silver.

As he entered, he walked down the gleaming halls ablaze with glowing light and came upon the throne room of the sun. Helios was waiting for him, for the sun sees everything. Golden beams flared from his crown and his eye twinkled with blazing light. Phaëthon trembled and explained why he had come.

Helios removed his crown and bade the young man to sit next to him. When the Sun God confirmed that he was indeed his father, he offered him anything he wanted. As a boy, he had always pretended to gallop through the heavens in the chariot of the sun god, imagining his father as he did so. And this was his request; he wanted to drive the golden chariot through the skies.

Helios warned him that it was difficult and dangerous, even for a god. The horses were wild and breathed fire. There are many other dangers along the sky's path like the Bull and the Scorpion and the Lion. But Phaëthon's mind was made up. Helios kept his promise warned his son to drive with care. He rubbed soothing ointment on his neck to protect him from the flames and told him to control the horses at all times, for they will try to run very high where you will scorch the heavens, or very low where you will scorch the earth.

But the eagerness of youth was more powerful, and the young man let the horses fly free and fast. Fire burned the earth and smoke blinded him. He could not regain the reigns. He cried out to have this unbearable experience end, and in his agony, Zeus heard his plea. He threw his thunderbolt at Phaëthon and struck him dead, thereby answering his plea.

Pathëon fell into a river and was found by sea nymphs, who buried him. As for Helios, he continues to drive his chariot even on days when he hides his sadness behind clouds and the storms of Zeus.

Orpheus and Eurydice

Orpheus was the son of Calliope, one of the nine Muses, by a mortal. His mother was the Muse of Music, and Orpheus was bestowed the gift of talent for playing the lyre. He played so sweetly that he was able to charm all the creatures of earth. The trees and flowers were captivated by this magnetism. Animals lay down tamed by the soothing sounds that came from his instrument, and even the streams changed the direction of their flow in order to follow him.

Orpheus fell in love with a young woman, Eurydice, also a mortal, who he married, but shortly after their wedding, she died tragically by a poisonous snake. So he roamed the earth in his grief singing and playing sad melodies. When he could no longer go on, he decided he would rather die than live without her, so he followed her into the underworld, where all the souls of the dead can be found. He reasoned that if he could charm everything on earth, perhaps he could also fascinate Hades, who would agree to release his beloved Eurydice.

He made his way into the underworld by going to the River Styx, the place where souls are carried to the gates of Tartaros. He played his lyre all along the way, enthralling the ferryman, the sea creatures and finally, Cerberus, the great three-headed dog who guards the entrance to Tartaros. He made his way through the long tunnels, down into the murky depths, still playing his lyre and listening to the sad wails of ghosts, the souls of the dead.

Hades and Persephone heard the gentle music, and the she begged the God of the Underworld to return Eurydice to her lover. Hades agreed, but as was usual in the ancient tales, there was always a condition. He told Orpheus that Eurydice was free to leave, but that she would walk behind you all the way out of the underground and that Orpheus was not to look back at her until they both reached the surface of the earth.

Up into the dark tunnels they went until at last Orpheus was able to see daylight. He called to Eurydice, but she did not hear him, so he turned around to find her and as he did so, she receded back into the dark tunnels crying, "Farewell". He tried to run after her, but the gods, though generous, do not allow second chances. He was not allowed back in and for the rest of his days, he wandered the earth singing sad songs.

Poor Misguided Oedipus

The Oracle at Delphi was used often by kings, queens, gods and divine creatures to look into the future so they could understand their fate in an attempt to deter an ill fate or prepare for a great one.

On this day, the oracle spoke to the King of Thebes, whose wife had just delivered a fine son into the world. The oracle told him that the boy would one day kill him and inherit his throne, so the king decided he could not let the boy live. He took the babe from its mother's arms and bound its feet together. Then he instructed his servant to take the infant to the mountains and leave it to die.

But shepherds who led their flocks to the mountains found the boy and carried it to their king, Polybus of Corinth who raised the child as though it were his own. He named the baby Oedipus which means "swollen foot", because his father had bound his feet and caused them to swell.

As Oedipus grew, he went to the Oracle at Delphi which told him he would kill his father and marry his mother. Oedipus was appalled by what he heard and claimed he would never kill his own father, thinking Polybus, the kind king was his father. But he knew the oracle was never wrong, to ensure his father's safety, he left the city of Corinth and went far, far away.

Soon he came to a crossroads where a chariot was passing. The driver demanded he move out of the way for his passenger was an important man, but Oedipus did not move. He believed himself to be the son of a king and therefore an important person, too. The man in the chariot became angry and ordered his driver to move on, and as the horses began to pull the chariot, it rode over the lame foot of Oedipus, who cried out in pain. He was so angered that he killed the driver and his important passenger, who turned out to be King Laius, his real father.

Now, Oedipus did not know who this man was, so he continued on his way to Thebes, where he met Queen Jocasta and married her. They lived happily for many years, but when a severe famine plagued the city, they turned to the Oracle at Delphi. The oracle told them to cast out the murderer who had killed King Laius and expel him from the land.

Now, there was an old blind seer who lived at the palace and he hurried to the throne room bearing news. The king and queen respected his wisdom and told him to speak what truth he had for them. So he told them what he knew, that King Oedipus was the killer of King Laius, your true father, and married your mother, Queen Jocasta.

In grief and horror, the queen killed herself, and Oedipus went mad. He blinded himself with a pin and removed himself from the castle, taking his daughter, Antigone, with him. Together they wandered the land until the day he died.

The Yoking of Atalanta and Hippomenes

In the ancient days, a baby, Atalanta, was cast into the woods to die because her father wanted a boy child, not a girl child. The baby was found and raised by a she-bear until the child grew strong and agile, able to hunt and fish and run in the woods. She took up with a band of hunters and roamed the free open air, living in the forest and loving the adventures each day brought.

She could shoot an arrow farther and with more accuracy than any man, and she could wrestle with the strongest. She could run faster and longer, and she was as independent and capable as any of her male counterparts.

King Iasus, her father, had abandoned her, but when he heard of her accomplishments, he wanted to claim his daughter as his own. He wanted her to come and live in the palace so he could display her like a trophy, for she was not only strong, but she was exceedingly beautiful. She agreed to live in the palace and finally the day came when the king wanted her to take a husband, but Atalanta wanted no part of marriage. She had no interest in taking a suitor.

But the king continued to invite many suitable men to convince her to marry. To Atalanta, they were all tiresome bores. The king was at a loss for what to do. He told his daughter that she must marry, so she said, "I will marry the man you can beat me in a foot race." She was confident that no man ever would. "And to all the men who lose, they will also lose their life." This, she felt, would discourage most of them from even trying.

The young prince, Hippomenes, decided to take his chance. He had fallen in love with Atalanta and when she met him, she was taken with him as well. She wanted him to win, but her pride would not let her throw the race. Hippomenes knew he had little chance of winning, so he prayed to the Goddess Aphrodite to help him.

She instructed him to take three golden apples and throw them to the ground to distract Atalanta. She will be intrigued by the apples and stop to pick them up. And so it was that Hippomenes threw the first apple and Atalanta stopped to pick up the beautiful golden fruit. Hippomenes now had the advantage, but Atalanta soon caught up and passed him by. As she did so, he threw the second apple out in front of her and she again stopped to pick it up. Once again, she was easily able to catch up to him. As the neared the finish line, he threw the last apple off to the side and into her view, hoping she would stop one last time and give him a chance to cross the line ahead of her.

But Atalanta did not want to lose the race, so Aphrodite intervened once more. She whispered in her ear, "That golden apple is the most precious of all and it came from my garden, picked for you alone."

With that, Atalanta crossed over to the apple, scooped it up and continued to run, but it was too late. Hippomenes had already won the race and cheers went up in the crowd! So the two were married and lived happily for a while, but they forgot the goddess who had helped them, so she changed one into a lion and the other into a lioness and yoked them together. They would spend their days pulling a chariot for a goddess.

Daedalus and Icarus

The great story of Theseus' triumph over the Minotaur in the Labyrinth created by Daedalus is told to us in the tale of the hero of Athens, whereby he killed the Minotaur and found his way out of the maze with the help of the king's daughter, Ariadne. King Minos, however, believed that he must have received help from Daedalus since he was the constructer of the maze and the only one who knew its secrets. So the king had Daedalus and his son,

Icarus, taken to the tower to be locked away forever.

Daedalus was a great architect and inventor, so devised a plan to escape the fate the king had set for him and his son by fashioning wings for them to fly from their prison. Each day, birds would rest on the ledge outside the high windows of the tower, and each day the two would collect their feathers. Soon they had enough to create great wings for each of them, and they set off. But Daedalus warned his impetuous son to keep to the middle wind. Too low and the wings would become damp and useless; too high and they would burn up from the sun.

"They spread their wings like gods and the boy, Icarus, tumbled through the air like an eagle, impatient to make a straight flight to safety. He ventured up and down, high and low, playfully gliding toward the sun and sea in a game to see how far he could go. But the wax on his wings had melted and he went down into the sea, lost forever."

Dionysus

Dionysus was the product of the God Zeus and his mortal lover, Semele, who was tricked by Hera into asking Zeus to reveal himself in his full godly form, knowing full well that no mortal could survive this sight. When she was burned by the sight of Zeus in his glory, the immortal god managed to pull Dionysus from the flames and save the boy, for was the child of a god and would himself be immortal.

But Hera was not pleased and arranged to have the baby killed by the Titans who ripped him apart, where upon he was saved and put back together by Rhea and sent to the mountains to be raised by nymphs. As he grew, he spread his wild ways throughout the woodlands where his followers either went mad in a fit of ecstasy or killed themselves in a state of frenzy.

He eventually became one of the most important gods because he was associated with rebirth and viticulture, the pruning of vines so they could grow more abundantly, and with the feeling that one was possessed of godly power upon taking wine. The festivals held in his honor are based in the new growth of spring and are often depicted in many Greek theatrical productions, where everyone who participated in the making of the production, including spectators, was considered a sacred servant of the God Dionysus.

Midas

Midas was a greedy king whose life revolved around his love of gold, and he spent much of his time counting his coins and assessing his wealth.

"Dionysus granted him one wish as repayment for his kind hospitality, and the greedy king requested that all he touched would turn to gold. And so, with fair warning against the consequences of such a wish, the God of

Wine kept his promise. In the morning, he was ecstatic as everything he touched did indeed become gold.

"But his happiness was short-lived, for when his beautiful daughter entered the room and hugged him, she too turned to gold and despair filled the heart of the king. Now a curse, he begged the god to remove this power, and Dionysus, being a good-hearted god, told him to wash his hands in the River Pactolus, where all gold flowed from him and everything he had heretofore touched returned to its original state."

Midas' life after that episode became one of a virtuous man, who took care of his people and led them to prosperity, so that when he died, they grieved for the king they adored.

The famous story of King Midas revolves around his ability to turn everything he touched into gold, and this is where we get the modern term "the Midas touch", used to refer to anyone who is successful in business transactions or to someone who has an easy time earning wealth.

Chapter 7: The Heroes

The stories of the heroes of Ancient Greece have been handed down orally and have been written about extensively in works by Homer, Hesiod and others, but these ancient heroes, like all heroes, inspire us to do better, to be better, to think of others before ourselves, and to have courage in the face of all obstacles. They are kings and commoners, mortals and demigods, and each trial gives a lesson in morality, making us dig deep into our own souls to find what integrity and strength we possess.

The Prophecy of Perseus

Perseus is perhaps the most illustrious of the Greek heroes, noted for his remarkable feats of bravery and his noble sense of morality. He believed his mortal half made him weak, but in the end he discovered that his human side is what made him stronger.

King Acrisius of Argos had visited the Oracle at Delphi and was told that this beautiful daughter, Danae would have a male child who would eventually kill him. The king knew the Oracle was always true, so he devised a plan to make certain that Danae never had any children. He locked her in a bronze house underground, where no man would ever see her, and in this way, he assured that she would never bear children.

But Zeus had other plans for Danae. There was a small patch of roof in the bronze house that allowed air and light to enter, and through this opening, Zeus entered in the form of gold fluttering down into her room. He declared his love for the girl and so it was that she bore Perseus, son of Zeus and the great-great grandfather of Heracles.

The king discovered her secret and told her that one day this boy would kill him, but because he is the son of Zeus, he could not take his life. He would not have that death on his hands for it would anger the mighty God of Thunder. So he locked them into an ark and threw them into the sea. If they died, he reasoned, it would be the fault of the God Poseidon. But unbeknownst to the king, the ark went aground and the two were rescued and cared for by a fisherman and his wife.

Perseus grew into a strong young man, who one day entered the games of the city, where his father had also gone to watch the games. He took his turn at throwing the discus, and when the wind took it, it blew into the crowd and struck his father, King Acrisius, and killed him. And so it was that the prophecy of the Oracle was fulfilled.

But Perseus would have many more adventures and challenges thrown at him before he returned with his future wife, Andromeda of Aethiopia, to what he considered his home on the Island of Serifos.

Perseus and Medusa

"And so it came to pass that Danae and the child, Perseus, came to set upon the coast of the Island of Serifos, where stand the palaces of two kings: Dictys and Polydectes. A fisherman found the ark on the coast and brought to the kindly king, Dictys, who allowed Danae to raise Perseus in the palace under his care. But Polydectes fell in love with Danae and he knew that Perseus, now a young man, would protect his mother's honor. And so the king announced he would marry Hippodameia, the daughter of King Oenomaus of Elis, for by deception, he would remove Perseus and put him in danger, assuring he would not return.

"The king asked for gifts of horses, knowing Perseus had none, so he bargained with him to bring him the head of the mortal Gorgon, Medusa, one of the three sisters. For this task, his marriage gift to the king would be fulfilled.

"Medusa, the mortal one, was a beautiful maiden who had spurned the great god Poseidon, and so he turned his wrath upon her and her sisters that whosoever would look upon them would be turned to stone. He covered their heads with snakes that writhed and spat, and though she kept her comely face, all else about her was monstrous.

"Perseus turned to Athena and Hermes for help and guidance, and together with the nymphs, they provided winged sandals to carry him to the end of the world and a cap that made him invisible. They made for him a sword and a mirrored shield to reflect the gorgon's gaze and in this way, he would not be turned to stone.

"When the head was cut, the blood spilled on the ground and from it came Pegasus, the winged horse, and Chrysaor, the winged boar. And Perseus took the head back to Polydectes, escaping the sisters, and the king gazed upon the face of Medusa and was turned to stone."

Perseus would later use the head to turn Atlas to stone and then Poseidon's mighty sea monster to whom Andromeda was being sacrificed.

Perseus and Atlas

"And so it was that Perseus made for home, and he had reached the western limit of the earth and needed rest, so he landed in the realm of King Atlas, the tale of which was told that he was a man of exceeding substance and his stature exceeded the height and bulk of all men. He was a man or wealth in flocks and orchards, gardens of great pride to him which held the golden drupe hidden among golden leaves.

"Perseus presented his lineage as the son of Zeus for an honorable opening to be welcomed as a guest, and his valiant triumph in the defeat of the Gorgon. But Atlas remembered the prophecy: a son of Zeus would come and take from him the golden apples, and so he decried the hero to leave under threat of peril.

"Perseus, knowing he could not battle the goliath, turned and drew the Gorgon's head from his bag and Atlas was turned to stone."

"But the indulgence of the Olympians was such that they increased Atlas' bulk to immense proportions. His parts became the trees and woods and cliffs all surrounding, while his head became the summit of the mountain and his bones were the rocks themselves. And all heaven and earth would rest upon his shoulders for eternity.

But Perseus was the not the son of Zeus who would steal the golden apples. That would be Heracles in his Eleventh Labor, aided by the guidance of Prometheus who he frees from the rock where he was being punished for gifting fire to mankind.

Perseus and Andromeda

Upon his journey back to Serifos, he came on the rock of the sea monster, where sacrifices were made to the beast, the pet of Poseidon, and there chained and bound to the rock with golden links was the beautiful Andromeda, princess daughter of Cepheus and Cassiopeia of Aethiopia.

In Cassiopeia's vanity, she thought her daughter more beautiful than any in the world and often boasted of the exquisite splendor of her velvet hair and shining eyes, her long sturdy limbs and skill with things of the home, for Andromeda had many womanly gifts and Cassiopeia thought her a girl to be paraded as a trophy.

"She is more beautiful even than all the daughters of Poseidon, the nymphs and the Nereids, the Amnisiades who care for the goddesses sacred deer. But Poseidon was angry at this mortal boasting and vowed to destroy the kingdom unless he sacrificed this lovely creature to Cetus, the monster of the deep.

"Stripped of her garments, her robes and her girdle, all but her jewels which shone into the sea and attracted the mighty Cetus, the golden chains held fast and Poseidon unleashed the beast to appease his anger.

"And in his flight, Perseus saw the lovely Andromeda who was doomed to fall for the pride of her mother. And he swooped down as the beast rose from the frothing sea, and with the sword of Hermes he slew the monster before the devouring of Andromeda and claimed her for his bride."

In some accounts of Perseus' saving of Andromeda, he draws the head of Medusa from his bag and turns the monster, Cetus, to stone. Often Cetus is mistaken to be the Kraken, a sea monster of Norse or Northern origin, but it's believed that they are two different creatures. However, Cassiopeia and Cepheus wished for a better union for their prize, their daughter, and so joined in secret with her former betrothed, Phineus, the king's brother to engage him in battle and kill the hero, Perseus.

"Phineus and his men prepared for the battle, thinking that Perseus had no armies to support and defend him, and he fought courageously though he was sorely outnumbered, and having been so outnumbered, he drew the head, the weapon, from his bag and turned the two hundred to stone."

In the end, safely back on the Island of Serifos, he gave his prize, the head of Medusa, to Athena to place it on her shield, and to the God Hermes he gave his winged sandals and cap and the magic mirror to honor the god.

The Twelve Labors of Heracles

Heracles was considered the strongest man in the world and is the other prominent hero in Greek mythology along with Perseus. He was a son of Zeus who had a mortal mother, Alcmene, a princess of Thebes. Hera, of course, was intolerant of her husband's philandering and so planned to have the babe killed. One night she sent two snakes to kill him in his sleep, but the baby grasped the snakes by their throats and strangled them. From then on, it was prophesied that Heracles would become a great hero of men and gods.

He became well trained in the bow and arrow, the sword and the hunt, but he had no interest in the finer side of life - poetry, literature and music - and inadvertently killed his music teacher by hitting him over the head with his lyre. He did not realize his strength and so to tame this part of his nature, he was sent away to the mountains where he would cause no trouble.

He grew strong and brave, and at the age of eighteen, he managed to kill a lion with his bare hands. But Hera's wrath would not be satiated. She was still angry and caused Heracles to go mad and kill his wife and children. In order to cleanse himself, he was ordered by the Oracle of Delphi to seek the counsel of Eurystheus, King of Mycenae. He must do whatever the king asked of him. And so it was that he was challenged by these great feats of strength and courage. These are the stories of the Labors of Heracles.

1. The Nemean Lion

"He shot the beast with arrows, whose skin was impervious to all manner of weapons, then wrestled it to ground, twisting its neck until it was dead. He ripped the skin from its body and wrapped himself in it as proof of his victory and for a token attribute. But the wrath of Hera was great and she would not be outdone, so she placed the spirit of the Lion amongst the stars for all eternity as proof of its greatness."

The Nemean Lion was the offspring of Typhon and Echidna and was set in the mountains of Nemea to plague the town and prey upon the tribes. Another version has the lion falling from the moon (Selene, Goddess of the Moon). "For I am sprung from fair-tressed Selene, who in a fearful shudder shook off the savage lion in Nemea, and brought him forth at the bidding of Queen Hera."

2. The Lernean Hydra

"The terrible Hydra rose from the murky waters, one head, then two, then more, each one more terrifying than the others. But one was the most terrible, for it alone was immortal and Heracles, using not strength but cunning, was sent to kill the beast. By the springs of Amymone, the Hydra cast its venom. Each time one head was destroyed, two more grew in its place. So brave Iolaus was summoned to burn the necks before they could burst forth with new heads. When all were destroyed, the final loathsome immortal head was chopped off and Heracles buried it under a rock."

Iolaus was a nephew of Heracles who often accompanied him during the Labors, but Eurystheus believed that because Heracles had help on this quest, it should not be counted, and so he added another labor to the ten.

3. The Ceryneian Hind

"The brazen deer had horns of gold and was as large as a bull. It was swift and hid for many days; for a whole year it managed to outrun Heracles, who remained undaunted. Finally, the animal stopped to drink from the river and Heracles saw his chance. He drew his bow, aimed, and with steady hand, shot the hind and carried it off.

The Third Labor was to capture the Hind of Cerynaea, the most favored pet of the Goddess Artemis. Eurystheus knew the animal was sacred and in this way he assured himself of getting rid of Heracles one way or another.

When Artemis appeared with Apollo at her side, she sought to punish Heracles, but he was truthful with her and told her of the command of the Oracle, so she softened and healed her pet, allowing Heracles to carry it live to the king.

4. The Erymanthean Boar

"The boar ran wild and its temper was high as it ran through Erymanthus terrorizing everything in its path. Heracles heard the creature before he saw it, for though it had the strength of a bull, it was a stupid animal and created a rash of noise as it ripped its tusks through men and beast alike. It snorted and stomped and Heracles chased it into a thicket where he could pierce it with his spear. He drove the wounded animal out into the open and netted it, then carried in on his shoulder to the palace."

Though this fourth labor did not seem as difficult to Heracles, Eurystheus, upon seeing Heracles carrying the live wounded boar, became frightened of his strength and hid himself out of sight.

5. The Augean Stables

"The supernatural oxen were driven in by the thousands and Heracles knew he would not be able to clean the stable in a day, as the Labor required. So he thought to use his wits rather than his strength. He dug two trenches thereby diverting the mighty rivers nearby into the stables and let the waters rush through, washing the stables clean."

The Fifth Labor was a task that was designed to defeat Heracles psychologically. The king soon realized that feats of strength were not challenging enough, so he sought to demoralize and humiliate Heracles. The stables were immeasurable and held thousands of cattle, goats and sheep of colossal proportions. Decades of dung filled the interior and Heracles recognized his own limitations. He went to King Augeas and "offered" to clean the stables in a single day if he would be rewarded with one tenth of the herd. The king agreed. However when Eurystheus found out he was paid for the task, he deemed it uncountable and added a twelfth labor to Heracles' penance.

6. The Stymphalian Birds

"The vicious man-eating creatures were equal to lions and leopards in their fierceness, and fly against all who come to hunt them. They tore at a man's armor with their mighty bronze beaks, and were covered with metallic feathers that could deflect an arrow. But the flesh beneath was not impervious to the arrow and, like a dragon, they had one vulnerable spot which lay at the back of the neck. So Heracles banged the bronze clappers forged by Hephaistos, God of the Forge, which were given to him by Athena, and scared the birds from their roost, upon which he was able to pierce each one at the back of the neck they flew."

To prove his success at this Sixth Labor, Heracles took several of the dead birds back to Eurystheus.

7. The Cretan Bull

Capturing the Cretan Bull was an easy task for Heracles, particularly after the first six Labors.

"The magnificent bull was sent forth from the loins of Poseidon to Minos, King of Crete, to prove he was worthy to be king, whereupon the mighty Olympian punished him for his deception in breaking his promise. His queen, Pasiphae, would be made to couple with the beast and bare the monster called Minotauros, which had the head of a bull and the body of a man. But the lamb of Poseidon was a gentle creature and easily captured by son of Zeus."

There are many stories that surround bulls in Greek mythology, and the Bull of Kretaios, the creation of Poseidon, was just one. To demonstrate how intricately these stories play out with each other, let's go back briefly to the story of Zeus and Europa, whom he tricked by disguising himself as a bull. Europa bore Minos, who would become the first King of Crete.

Minos, in order to prove his right to rule, promised Poseidon he would sacrifice any creature the Sea God sent to him, but when the god sent the beautiful bull, Minos replaced it with another. Poseidon's wrath caused the bull to rampage all over Crete, and this is where we see our hero, Heracles, become involved during this, his Eighth Labor.

When he successfully delivered the bull to Eurystheus, the bull was set free only to be driven to Marathon where it once again began to terrorize the villages and was eventually destroyed by another hero, Theseus.

In the meantime, Poseidon caused Minos' wife, Pasiphae to fall in love with the magnificent bull sent by the God of the Sea and she bore another monster, the Minotaur, who would be imprisoned in the Labyrinth where, once again, the hero Theseus would come to the rescue and slay the beast.

8. The Mares of Diomedes

"Heracles entered into the Eighth Labor, whereupon he was sent to the kingdom of Diomedes, a son of Ares, who was possessed of four man-eating mares. Heracles sailed to the city of Mykenai (Mycenia) and seeing the great beasts chained by irons to a trough of brass, and eating the limbs of travelers, he devised a plan to overpower the grooms, release the horses and drive them back to Eurystheus. And so it was that he fed to them the beast master, the King of the Bistones, and in doing so, satiated them."

When Heracles returned with the mares, he dedicated them to Hera. The foolish Eurystheus let the mare go free, and they found their way to Mount Olympus where their line continued in greatness. The legends claim that these were the same horses ridden in the Trojan War by Alexander the Great.

9. The Girdle of Hippolyte

"The great Amazon Warriors put on their armor and mounted their steeds, ready to defend their queen, for Hera, disguised as one of them, walked among the ranks and rallied them to battle. Heracles, upon seeing the charging women in full armor and carrying weapons, knew he had to kill Hippolyte and thus end the battle before it began. Thus he took the belt and returned it to Eurystheus, fulfilling the Ninth Labor."

Once again, we see Hera trying to thwart Heracles, who had in fact told Hippolyte, Queen of the Amazons, the truth of the Oracle. She in turn was willing to give him the belt. But as fate would have it, Hera's interference caused the unnecessary death of Hippolyte.

10. The Cattle of Geryon

"Helios, the Sun God, saw fit to help Heracles as he crossed to the far ends of the earth in search of the cattle of the monster, Geryon. These were ordinary cattle, but the monster was fearsome and the herd was guarded by a two headed dog as large as the beasts of Tartaros. A battle ensued and Heracles slew Geryon and the dog with his arrows."

For his Tenth Labor, Heracles was bound to steal the Cattle of Geryon, a monster of great proportions and a grandson of Medusa the Gorgon, with three torsos and three heads above one set of bulging muscular legs.

Apparently, Heracles was doomed to meet trials wherever he went because although he was able to steal the cattle, once again Hera interfered, this time on his journey home. After battling and killing three sons of Poseidon who attempted to steal the cattle, a bull who got into the mix and caused him more trouble, and a king who deterred him and was ultimately slain, the goddess sent a gadfly to bite at the herd and scatter them, sending our hero on a mission to regather them so he could present them to Eurystheus.

11. The Apples of the Hesperides

"Heracles ventured through all the lands, battling with Ares the God of War and Nereus who rose from the sea, and freeing Prometheus from his fate, until finally he approached Ladon, the hundred-headed dragon who guarded the apples, and the Hesperides who were the daughters of the mighty Atlas, the Titan who held up the earth and sky."

Heracles spent more than eight years fulfilling the Labors, making amends for the mad killing of his wife and children, an act which was provoked in him by the Goddess Hera. But because two of the labors were deemed unaccountable by Eurystheus, Heracles was bound to perform two more labors.

The Eleventh Labor sees Heracles on a quest to find the golden apples of Zeus, a wedding gift from the Goddess Hera which he kept in a secret garden at the farthest and northernmost edge of the world, but Heracles had no idea where they were until he meets Prometheus chained to a rock where he was being punished for gifting fire to mankind. Heracles frees him and in return, Prometheus tells him where to find the golden apples.

12. Cerberus, the Guard of Hades

"Heracles came at last to the entrance of Tartaros, where the beast lay in wait. It had three heads, wild and frothing, snapping and snarling, and a serpent tail that spit its deadly venom. It was Cerberus, the hound of Hades."

In the Twelfth and final labor, Heracles is ordered to bring Cerberus, the vicious three headed dog who guards the underworld, back to

Eurystheus, a journey from which no mortal had ever returned.

Heracles, having learned that truth is mightier than the sword, made his way to Tartaros and asked the god for Cerberus. Hades agreed to give him the monster if he could overpower it with nothing more than his bare hands. And so it was that Heracles wrestled the mighty beast to the ground and conquered it, bringing it to Eurystheus who then returned it to its rightful place guarding the gates of Hades.

Jason and the Argonauts: The Golden Fleece

The adventures of Jason, son of King Aeson of Iolcus, and his Argonauts have been retold in modern times in movies and books as an epic tale of bravery and revenge, and this hero has been romanticized as much as Heracles, Perseus and Zeus himself.

His uncle was Pelias, who had overthrown their father the king, so Jason's mother took him away to keep him safe. He was raised by the kindly centaur, Chiron, and to this end, he was able to grow into a strong and capable young man.

But Pelios had consulted the Oracle who told him that he would be slain by a member of his family, a man with one sandal, and so it was that Jason returned to the palace to claim his thrown. Pelios would only yield under one condition, however; that Jason retrieve the Golden Fleece, which Pelios claimed to be the rightful property of the kingdom of Iolcus.

So Jason chose a group of fine brave men and had a ship built by Argus, a master shipbuilder. It had fifty oars and fifty men to row. These were the famed Argonauts, so called after the name of the ship, the *Argo*. Among those men was Heracles, the hero of the Twelve Labors.

"The Argo sailed for many days through the black waters of the roiling seas and at last anchored in Colchis where the Fleece was guarded by a fierce dragon. As the Argonauts rested, Hera and Athena watched from Mount Olympus, and with the aid of Aphrodite, they caused Medea, a witch, to fall in love with Jason, knowing that she was the only one who could help him through his dangerous mission."

But when Jason and his men reached the palace of King Aeëtes who had possession of the fleece, a bargain was struck: Jason must perform a seemingly impossible task in exchange for the Golden Fleece.

"You must yoke to a plow two bulls that breathe fire and then plow a field into furrows into which you will sow the teeth of a dragon from which armed men will grow. When they attack you, you alone must destroy them."

Jason agreed to perform the task, and at that moment, Eros flew down and shot a love arrow into Medea's heart, causing her to fall in love. She was the daughter of Aeëtes and therefore reluctant to help her father's enemy, but in the end, she gave Jason a magic ointment, telling him to spread it over his body and his weapons to protect him from the fire-breathing bulls and the armed men who would spring from the dragon's teeth. She also gave him a magic stone.

"When the bulls were set loose, fire rained in the field, and Jason, being protected by Medea's ointment, took hold of their mighty horns and threw them to the ground, and yoking them to the plow, drove deep furrows into the land and sprinkled it with the teeth of the dragon, which gave forth a fierce army of warriors who sprang at him. He threw Medea's rock among them and they began to battle among themselves."

But when the battle was won, Aeëtes made a new plan to have his armies attack Jason when he came to claim the fleece, so Medea, being a sorceress, knew her father's plan and warned Jason to take the fleece by night, before her father attacked. And so it was that the *Argo* slipped near the shore of the sacred grove where the shimmering fleece was kept hanging from a tree, gleaming under the light of the moon. The dragon which guarded it hissed and spat, so Medea, singing a lullaby, soon put the beast to sleep. And so the fleece was won.

But Medea had no power to hold Jason's love and he married another. He was put out of favor with the gods by breaking his oath and he died an old man. As he sat beside the decaying *Argo* remembering his glory days, the old ship screeched and moaned as it swayed on the lonely shore. Jason was tired and so asked Zeus to show mercy on him, whereupon a lashing snapped and the hull crushed him, ending his life and making him a legend.

The Golden Fleece hung in the temple of Zeus for all to remember the heroic feats of Jason and his Argonauts.

According to Appolonius and the library at Alexandria, the crew of the Argo is indefinite. Pedigrees were handed down and so the son of an original crew member would also lay claim to this title, making it almost impossible to trace the original crew members. The following list is collated from several lists given in ancient sources.

This was the crew of the *Argo:*

Acastus

Actor, son of Hippas

Admetus

Aethalides

Amphiaraus

Amphidamas

Amphion, son of Hyperasius

Ancaeus, son of Poseidon

Ancaeus, son of Lycurgus

Areius

Argus, builder of the Argo

Argus, Son of Phrixus

Ascalaphus

Asclepius

Asterion, son of Cometes

Asterius, brother of Amphion

Augeas

Autolycus, son of Deimachus

Bellerophon

Butes

Calais, son of Boreas

Caeneus, son of Coronus

Canthus

Cepheus, King of Tegea

Castor, son of Tyndareus, brother of Pollux

Cytissorus

Clytius, son of Eurytus

Deucalion of Crete

Echion

Eribotes

Erginus, son of Poseidon

Erytus, brother of Echion

Euphemus

Euryalus

Eurydamus

Eurymedon, son of Dionysus

Eurytion

Eurytus, son of Hermes

Heracles, son of Zeus

Hippalcimus

Hylas

Idas

Idmon

Iolaus, nephew of Heracles

Iphitos

Jason

Laërtes, father of Odysseus

Laokoön, brother of Oeneus

Leitus

Leodocus

Lynceus

Melas

Meleager

Mopsus

Menoetius

Nauplius

Neleus, son of Poseidon

Nestor

Oileus

Orpheus

Palaemon

Palaimonius, son of Hephaestus

Peleus

Peneleos

Periclymenus, grandson of Poseidon

Phalerus

Phanus, brother of Staphylus and Eurymedon

Poeas

Philoctetes

Phlias, son of dionysus

Phocus

Phrontis

Prias, brother of Phocus

Pollux, son of Zeus

Polyphemus

Staphylus

Talaus

Telamon

Thersanon, son of Helios and Leucothoe

Thesus, son of Poseidon

Tiphys

Zetes, son of Boreas

The Ten Year Voyage of Odysseus

Odysseus played a part in several stories including the story of the Trojan War, the Land of the Lotus Eaters, the Island of the Cyclops, the Island of the Winds, and more.

After his victory at Troy in the Trojan War, Odysseus set sail for home, but the gods were angry for they had aided him in his battles and he did not offer his thanks to them. And so it was that Athena enlisted the aid of Poisedon to unleash a violent tempest to toss the Greek's ships on their way homeward. Many of Odysseus' ships were lost in the raging storms, but the ship that carried Odysseus was spared, though it was driven far off its course. When at last land was sighted, the men rested and ate of the fruit that grew on the trees and bushes.

"Odysseus was sorely dismayed by his men, who ate of the fruit, for this was the Land of the Lotus Eaters, whose trees bore the sweet delicacies that relieved men of their memories and all desire to return home. To this end, Odysseus had to drag each man and tie him securely, for they would not follow him voluntarily. Then they set sail for home.

Next, Odysseus and his men land on the Island of the Cyclopes. This is the Island of Serifos, the same island that Perseus and Danae landed on in their ark, and the island where Perseus was raised.

"Once again, the ships needed to stop, this time for fresh water, and it happened that they landed on the Island of the Cyclopes, giants with one eye in their foreheads who lived wild in the caves and mountains.

"When Odysseus and his men entered the cave, there they found an abundance of cheese and milk, for the Cyclopes were herders of sheep and stored their food in caves. This was the cave of Polyphemus, a son of Poseidon and the most savage of the giants. When the giant returned, he feasted on some of the men, and clever Odysseus then thrust a spear into his one eye as he slept.

"The horrible giant awoke, but the men had tied three sheep abreast and each clung to their undersides so the giant would not feel them as he let his sheep leave the cave. And so it was that they escaped, but as they sailed away, Odysseus shouted his name to the Cyclops so Polyphemus would know who blinded him."

Unfortunately, Polyphemus was a son of Poseidon, so once again our hero and his men are plagued by the vengeance of the God of the Sea. This time, he put in at the Island of the Winds where he was given a bag that contained the violent winds and tempests. He was told not to look inside, but when he fell into a deep sleep after nine days at sea, the curiosity of his men caused them to look inside the bag, thereby releasing the winds and scattering the ships.

As they made their way through the churning waters, all the ships but Odysseus' harbored into a savage island where the inhabitants killed them all and destroyed their ships. Only Odysseus and the men on his ship were spared, for they had stayed out to sea.

And so it was that Circe the sorceress led them to an island filled with shady trees and a sumptuous palace. Surely they would partake of some kind hospitality there. But as they neared the palace, they were surrounded by wolves and tigers, who had once been men but were under the spell of Circe.

A great feast was set before them in the palace hall and soon they became sleepy from the enchanted wine, and Circe turned them all into pigs and shut them up in a pen.

As it happened, one man, Eurylochus, had remained outside the palace and saw what had happened, so he ran to the ship and warned Odysseus. Our hero would rescue his men, as you will see, and as he walked to the palace, a youth appeared. It was the God Hermes who warned him of Circe's sorcery. Hermes gave Odysseus a flower that would protect him, and this is how he was able to threaten Circe within an inch of her life if she did not return his men to their original state. Eventually, they left the island, but not before Circe, who had promised not to hurt them in exchange for her life, gave Odysseus some advice.

"And so it was that Odysseus visited the underworld alone seeking the counsel of the seer, Teiresias, who would tell him of the fate that awaited him on the rest of his journey."

"The Sirens call to men and entice them with their songs and causing them to jump to their deaths into the sea, to be lost forever."

The men were instructed to put wax in their ears, but Odysseus wanted to hear the songs of the Sirens, so he told his men to tie him securely to the mast and ignore all pleas to release him until the shipped had passed out of danger.

Next, the ship would have to pass through the narrow strait guarded by the monsters Scylla and Charybdis, who threw the massive boulders together to smash any ships that attempted to cross the strait. One of the men were snatched by Scylla, with her six heads, and as she ate him, the ship sailed through and away from the danger.

And finally, remembering the warning of the seer, Odysseus warned his men of the next impending danger. They were not to eat of the cattle of Helios when they landed on the Island of the Sun. Unfortunately, the winds were unfavorable and they were stranded there for 30 days. Soon their food ran out and they began to hunt the cattle. Helios was outraged and enlisted Zeus to destroy the men and their ships. All perished except Odysseus who lashed himself to a mast and drifted to the Island of Calypso, the sea nymph, where he spent many years. Zeus took pity on him and with the aid of Calypso, was able to build a raft, but once again, Poseidon shattered the tiny craft and Odysseus landed on another island, the home of King Alcinoüs, who gave him a sturdy ship to sail home.

At last, after ten years, he arrived home, alone and saddened by the loss of so many of his men. But his troubles were not over. His wife Penelope was to choose the winner of an archery contest as her new husband, for she thought surely Odysseus was dead. So the Goddess Athena turned him into an old beggar to fool his enemies, the other suitors who vied for his throne, and he won the contest, regaining his throne and his wife.

Theseus and the Minotaur

Theseus was the son of King Aegeus and Princess Aethra who were secretly married, and he grew up not knowing who is father was. He was the cousin of Heracles, and upon his sixteenth birthday, he was given a task that would enable him to find out the identity of his father. He was told to roll away a rock which hid a sword and sandals, place there by King Aegeus, whom Theseus was now to claim as his father.

So he took the long road to Athens. But Medea the sorceress, as you will recall from the story of Jason and the Golden Fleece, was the daughter of Aegeus, and knew of Theseus' coming, so she told the king that he was planning to dethrone him. But when he presented the sword revealed to him, Aegeus knew this was indeed his son.

Every nine years, the people of Athens sacrificed seven youths and seven maidens to King Minos of Crete to appease the beastly Minotaur, but before the final lot was drawn,

Theseus volunteered to kill the Minotaur and end the sacrifices.

"When the ship arrived in Crete, Ariadne, the king's daughter, became smitten with Theseus, who returned her love. She crept to the chambers where the youths and maidens were kept telling the guards she was there to comfort them, and upon gaining entrance, she gave Theseus a ball of twine which he could post by the gate of the Labyrinth, and in this way he could follow it back and find his way out.

"When he entered the gates of the Labyrinth, the Minotaur was asleep. The tunnels were in blackness with no light to guide his path, so he was made to feel his way along the twisting winding passages into the Labyrinth, where at any moment he might stumble upon the sleeping beast. He moved quietly, listening for the sound of its heavy breath; the low rumbling in its throat. As it grew louder, his head ached from the sound, but still he moved on toward the dreadful Minotaur, whose nostrils spewed out fire.

"Theseus strangled the beast where he lay and followed the twine back to the gates of the Labyrinth where he returned to his homeland."

Ariadne had been waiting for him at the gates, and when he came out safely, she and the other thirteen meant for the sacrifice boarded the ship to Athens along with Theseus, but Dionysus came to him and warned him to leave her on the island of Naxos, for the god loved Ariadne. And so it was that she was left alone. When the ship reached the shores of Athens, the king thought the fourteen had perished and so threw himself off a cliff into the sea and drowned. To this end, Theseus became king of Athens, but he had no desire to rule. He left the people to rule themselves, creating the first true democracy, and he was remembered as a wise hero of the people.

Achilleus and Thetis

Achilles (Achilleus) is the son of the sea goddess Thetis and Peleus, a mortal. Thetis is foretold by the Goddess Themis that her son would die in battle, so she holds her baby boy by the heel of his foot and dips him into the River Styx, the Holy River of Invincibility. Because Thetis can see the fate of her son but is helpless to do anything about it, she is constantly strained by his unwillingness to heed her warnings. She continually tells him of impending danger, and although aware of his fate, he chooses his own path, a path of glory and action over any consequences that might come of them.

"In turn the goddess Thetis of the silver feet answered him [Akhilleus]: Yes, it is true, my child this is no cowardly action, to beat aside sudden death from your afflicted companions. Yet, see now, your splendid armor, glaring and brazen, is held among the Trojans. Yet I think he [Hektor] will not glory for long, since his death stands very close to him. Therefore do not yet go into the grind of the war god, not before with your own eyes you see me come back to you. For I am coming to you at dawn and as the sun rises bringing splendid armor to you from the lord Hephaistos." (Homer, Iliad 18. 127 ff)

Thetis often conferred and pleaded with Zeus to protect her beloved son, but Zeus seemed uninterested in her cause for one simple reason: The Oracle stated that Thetis would bear a son who would command more admiration from the people than Zeus himself. In order to change that destiny, he had her marry a mortal so as to diminish or water down the power of her generation.

Peleus was chosen who was a king of Thessaly. Zeus instructed him in the way to capture her. She had the power to change shapes at will, so Peleus was to hold onto waylay her and hold onto her as she morphed, until such time as she became placated, then they would marry. And so it was that she bore the son, Akhilleus.

During the great war between the Greeks and the Trojans, she enlisted the help of many gods and goddesses to help her son, many of whom she had helped when they were found in a crisis at sea. Even Zeus was bound to return a favor, for when the Olympians had sought to bind him in chains and dethrone him, she called upon Briareus (Aegaeon), the Hekatonkheire, to aid her in dissuading them and securing Zeus' release.

And so it was that the great hero, Achilles, led a short life of glory rather than a long one that would have been without the fame of his heroics. He died on the battlefield at Troy, but not before destroying many numbers of towns and warriors in the battle to defend the Greek armies.

Chapter 8: The Battles

The epic battles that took place in the stories of Greek mythology were sometimes based on real wars, but whether real or not, they were filled with heroes of great courage who performed amazing feats of daring and strength, and who, against all odds, prevailed against their enemies.

The Titanomachy

The Titanomachy was the first great battle between the Titans, the first children of the primeval gods who fought from Mount Othrys, and the mighty Olympians, the next generation of the primeval gods.

The Titan Gods included the twelve Uranides (Cronus, Oceanus, Iapetus, Hyperion, Crius, Coeus, Rhea, Tethys, Theia, Phoebe, Themis and Mnemosyne) and the four Iapetionides (Atlas, Prometheus, Epimetheus and Menoetius).

The battle between Cronus and the sons of Cronus lasted ten years, until finally Gaea promised the victory to Zeus if he would retrieve her children, the Hecatoncheires and the Cyclopes, from Tartarus where they were cast by Cronus.

When the Titans were defeated, they were thrown into a cavity below Tartarus and the first children of Gaea were set to guard them.

As was the custom with titles, the honor of being called a Titan followed the children of Titans. These included Prometheus, Hecate, Latona, Pyrrha, Helios, and Selene and their descendants. So the race lived on, but the original Titans were banished forever.

The Fight of the Gigantes

There is often confusion that surrounds the Fight of the Gigantes (Gigantomachy) and the Titanomachy. The Titanomachy was fought with the Titans against the Olympians for rule of the universe, with the Cyclopes and

Hekatonkhieres variously taking sides. The Gigantomachy was allegedly the result of the violation (rape) of Hera, the Olympian wife of Zeus, King of the Olympian gods, by either Eurymedon or Porphyrion (depending on the source), both Giants. This war was fought with the Giants on one side against all the other gods: Titans, Olympians, demi-gods, and even Heracles.

The Gigantes were a tribe of Giants, the children of Gaia by either Tartaros or the castrated Ouranos (Heaven), and their similarity to the Hekatonkhieres is likely the source of the confusion. However, according to various writers, they were not large or gigantic in stature, but in nature, and were likely born after the Titans.

"The sons of Gaia appeared dressed in full armor, wielding spears of fire forged from the earth, and the skins of the giant cats, throwing rocks that no man could carry. The mountains roared and spewed its molten breath as the might Olympians crashed through the gates, bearing with them Heracles of great fame.

"Etna and Vesuvius did rain upon the land and the strength of the aggressors grew, and all the offspring of the gods lay into the giants with their gifts: the arrow, the thunderbolt, the sheaf, the seas, and the wind.

"Yet still the foot soldiers of Gaia came by the hundreds with all of their excesses of violence, arrogance and pride, hurling rocks as large as a mountain. And the vengeance of the Olympians would cause them to suffer unforgettable punishments for the evil they did upon Hera, and they were vanquished to live buried under the volcanoes of Mother Earth where could do no harm."

The Gigantomachy was the second great battle for divine control of the universe. The Greek scholar Apollodorus writes that perhaps it was revenge on the part of Gaia that motivated the war because the Titans and then the Olympians had imprisoned her other children, the Cyclopes and the Hekatonkeires. He also suggests as a motive the Olympians' vanquishing of the Titans in the Titanomachy.

Names for the Giants can be found in ancient literary sources and inscriptions, with references to more than seventy entries. They are also found on numerous antiquities and depictions of battles including paintings, vases, cups, and buildings such as the Siphnian Treasury at Delphi. Here is a condensed list of some of the Giants identified by Harvard University's Center for Hellenistic Studies.

Agrius: Killed by the Moirai (Fates) with bronze clubs.

Alcyoneus: He was the greatest of the Giants along with Polydorus; killed by Heracles.

Alektos/Allektos: Named on the late sixth century Siphnian Treasury and the second century BC Pergamon Altar.

Aristaeus: According to the Suda, he was the only Giant to "survive" the war.

Astarias/Aster/Asterius/Asterus: Mentioned in the epic poem Meropis as an invulnerable warrior killed by Athena, who flays him and uses his impenetrable skin for her shield.

Clytius: Killed by Hecate with her torches.

Enceladus: Crushed by Athena under Mount Etna on the Island of Sicily.

Ephialtes Blinded by arrows from Apollo and Heracles.

Euryalus: He is seen fighting the god Dephaestos.

Eurymedon: King of the Giants who "brought destruction on his people" He was possibly the Eurymedon who was the cause of the war by raping Hera, producing Prometheus.

Eurytus: Killed by Dionysus with his staff.

Gration: Killed by Artemis.

Hapladamas: Speared by Apollo while attacking Zeus; may have been enlisted by the Titan, Rhea.

Hippolytus: Killed by Hermes who was wearing the helmet of Hades which made its wearer invisible.

Lion: Mentioned as a giant who was challenged to single combat by Heracles and killed. Lion-headed Giants are shown on the Gigantomachy frieze of the second century BC Pergamon Altar.

Mimas/Mimos/Mimon: Killed by Hephaestus or burned by a thunderbolt of Zeus.

Pallas: Flayed by Athens who used his skin as a shield.

Pelorus: Killed by Ares.

Polybotes: Crushed under Nisyros, a piece of the island of Kos broken off and thrown by Poseidon.

Porphyrion: With Alcyoneus, he is considered the greatest of the Giants; he attacked Heracles and Hera, but was smote by Zeus with a thunderbolt, and Heracles shot him dead with an arrow."

Thoas/Thoon: Killed by the Moirai (Fates) with bronze clubs.

The Trojan War

The long war between the Greeks and the Trojans began because of a quarrel between three goddesses, and it went something like this:

The Goddess Eris, the Goddess of Discord, was upset because she had not been invited to a wedding between a king and a sea nymph, so she decided to cause some trouble at the banquet. She threw an apple into the crowd upon which she had written: *For the fairest*. Each of three goddesses, Athena, Aphrodite and Hera believed the apple was intended for them, and so they began to fight over it. Zeus knew that someone had to decide who should be the rightful owner of the apple, but because Hera was his wife and could become ill-tempered, he did not want to make that decision.

He enlisted the aid of a youth named Paris. Zeus told them to go to Mount Ida and seek out the youth who would decide which of them was the fairest. But Paris was tricked by the Goddess Aphrodite who promised him the most beautiful woman in all the world if he judged her to be the fairest. But Helen of Troy, the most beautiful woman in the world, was the wife of the King of Sparta. So Aphrodite arranged for Helen to fall in love with Paris and together they fled to Troy.

"And so it was that a plan was devised to gain the fortified walls of Troy and recapture Helen. The men climbed into the hollow belly of the great wooden horse, one by one, first Odysseus and then the rest, and one man, Sinon, stood behind to bring the gift and convince the

Trojans to bring the horse inside the gates by making them believe it was a gift for Athena.

"All was quiet, for the men of Troy had celebrated greatly with wine, and now they slept soundly. The trap door opened and one by one, Odysseus and his men crept among the men and killed them all. Then they signaled to the rest of the Greek army who entered the gates and there ensued a terrible battle in which the Greeks were victorious and Helen was returned to her husband, Menelaus."

However Homer's Iliad tells the story a bit differently.

Our hero, Achilles, like many Greek heroes and gods, is depicted as a man who is vulnerable, strong and often stubborn, who sometimes makes decisions that are rash and founded in emotion rather than reason. When his friend, Patroclus, was slain, Achilles was said to be "seized with unspeakable grief", but we don't know if that grief came from the loss of his friend or the fact that Achilles was lying in his tent, stubbornly refusing to take any further participation in the war, an act that stemmed from a dispute over a woman. Likely it was his guilt that spurred him on.

"Achilles now rose, and his thundering voice alone put the Trojans to flight... [He] hurried to the field of battle, disdaining to take any drink or food until the death of his friend should be avenged. (Homer xix. 155, & c.) He wounded and slew numbers of Trojans (xx. xxi.), and at length met Hector [the bulwark of the Trojans], whom he chased thrice around the walls of the city. He then slew him, tied his body to his chariot, and dragged him to the ships of the Greeks. (xxii.) After this, he burnt the body of Patroclus, together with twelve young captive Trojans, who were sacrificed to appease the spirit of his friend."

"And so it was that the death of Achilles was mourned by gods and men, that he was buried in a golden urn given as a gift to Thetis from Dionysus, and a mound raised over his burial spot on the coast of Hellespont."

It's sometimes easy and sometimes difficult to sympathize with Achilles. He seems to be a loving son and a good friend, a fierce and fearless warrior who also loves a peaceful home life. His downfall is his ambition, and he is often led by his emotions and pride, making him relentless in his revenge.

Most people would not consider killing or sacrificing twelve young soldiers to appease God or the spirit of a dead friend killed in battle. So whether you agree with the idea of war or not, the concept of a hero in this regard conflicts with our sense of right and wrong, although many today often seek revenge for a perceived offense.

The Myth of Er

Although the Myth of Er is not a battle in the physical sense of the word, it represents the battle in which the soul must partake between this world and the next and illustrates the ancient Greek idea of reward and punishment in this life and the next.

The story is of part of Plato's *Republic*, but the word *myth* in this sense is used to mean *account*.

The story tells of a man named Er who dies in battle and is resurrected 12 days after his death, his body completely intact, to give his account of his journey into the afterlife with an unprecedented look at the celestial spheres of the astral plane, something we might see as analogous to the layers of an onion, each in contact with the next layer, growing larger toward the outer positions.

Naturally, the ancients were mystified by what they saw as being the intermediary between earth and heaven, and these layers were believed to be the domain of angels, a theosophy that would influence religion and philosophy for many centuries.

Plato's story solidifies the concept that people are rewarded or punished in the next life based on their performance in this one.

Er tells the story of four judges sitting at the entrance to the sky and the ground directing the souls of the dead on a path that led either to the sky or below the earth. But Er was instructed to return to tell his story and his experience for all mankind to hear that they should know and be aware of their behavior on Earth.

Each soul which has not reached the wisdom of moderation, or what Eastern philosophy refers to as enlightenment, is assigned a guardian or spirit to return to a new life on earth, and in doing so, it is explained, the soul is immortal and cannot die. We can choose our next life and in this, our character is revealed. The goal is to grow spiritually in wisdom, courage and virtue as expressed in our daily lives, not just our intellect.

This philosophy is clear in the many stories of ancient Greek gods and heroes, for no matter what is thrown at them or how many challenges they must face, the heroes exemplify the way we should live in order to experience heavenly reward. Those who fail the test and are punished by the gods must somehow find a way to make amends or "learn their lesson".

Even the idea that as the generations of gods moved forward, each took on the attributes of the former, and so it is with the soul. We are to remember how we lived in our past lives and improve upon that to a virtuous end. The "old soul" is one who has returned many times and perhaps can't seem to get it right. In the story of Er, we are made to understand that reaching a higher plane, not physically but spiritually, we can replace the cycle of reward and punishment with a consciousness that is even greater than the Greek gods, who are seen as powerful but not faultless.

And so the "battle" between good and evil rages on, continually trying to influence the souls of men, but man himself is the only force which ultimately makes the decision about his path.

Chapter 9: Monsters and Hybrids

The ancient land, seas and skies produced many strange hybrids; human-animal forms, monsters and magical creatures that feature prominently in Greek mythology. These creatures fall into the Seventh Class of Immortals. They were considered semi-divine creatures who were used by the gods to implement many of their punishments and rewards on humans, and to test the loyalty, courage and mettle of mortals.

Giants were of two types; those such as the Cyclopes were like men, but far greater in size, and one might include Antaeus and Orion. The superhuman giants are those who warred with the gods such as Tityus who "stretched out over the plain covering nine acres", and Enceladus who "required the whole of Mount Aetna to be laid upon him to keep him down".

Briareus and Typhon were giants who could put the gods to fear for they were formidable enemies who were finally subdued by the thunderbolts created by the Sea Goddess, the Immortal who taught the Cyclopes to make the thunderbolt of Zeus.

If a monster was combined of two animals, both the qualities of those animals were attributed, and they were beings of immensely unnatural proportions usually regarded with terror because of their mammoth strength and ferocity..

Amalthea: Amalthea wasn't actually a monster or a hybrid, but a goat which bears mentioning as part of the grand scheme of the life of Zeus. When Cronus began eating his children one by one, Rhea gave him a large rock to eat, telling him it was her last-born, Zeus. But she took the baby Zeus to a cave to be raised under the care of the goat, Amalthea, who nursed him and nourished him until he was grown.

As a child, he played with the goat, and one day unintentionally broke off her horn, for which he made amends by blessing the broken horn and turning it into a horn of abundance from which Amalthea could find anything she desired. The Horn of Amalthea or the Horn of Plenty is often referred to as the Cornucopia, an eternal symbol of abundance.

Centaur: The Centaur had the head, arms and torso of a man and the body and legs of a horse. They might be good or evil.

Cerberus: Cerberus was a three headed dog that guarded the underworld, Tartaros. This monster was another offspring of Typhon and Echidna and the Twelfth Labor of Hercules.

Charybdis: A sea monster who drew created whirlpools by pouring large amounts of water from her mouth to prevent ships from moving through the narrow passage guarded by the two monsters, Charybdis and Scylla.

Chimera: A fire breathing monster with the head of a lion, the body of a goat, and the tail of serpent, who was killed by Bellerophon.

"Pegasus rode high and mighty in the sky with brave Bellerophon on his back. The Chimera paced below them, jumping from rock to rock, roaring fire blazing from its mouth. Out of the fields it sprang and seemed to be a dream to Bellerophon. Then he moved swiftly, with leaded spear. As Pegasus circled the monster, he thrust it deep into the mouth of the Chimera, whose fire melted the leaden tip, pouring it down her throat and killing her."

Chiron: Chiron was the son of Kronos and Philyra, a nymph. He was notable as a healer who learned his skills of music, prophecy, poetry, and healing under the tutelage of the God Apollo. This is the kindly Centaur who took the place of Prometheus on his rock under the bargain made by Zeus, who gave Prometheus the opportunity to be saved under two conditions:; an Immortal must volunteer to take his place and a mortal must unchain Prometheus and kill the eagle that was eating his liver. As a student of Chiron, one day Heracles accidentally wounded the Centaur with an arrow, and being immortal, the wound stood fast, so the kindly beast agreed to take the place of Prometheus.

"The centaurs were wild and uncivilized, but one emerged with all the intellect and reason of a man who was faithful to the gods. Chiron was his name and when he was struck down by a poisoned arrow of Heracles, Zeus saw fit to distinguish him among the stars so that his eternal existence might be seen by all."

Giant Serpent: Serpents were often called dragons and this one guarded the sacred spring at Thebes. It was the offspring of Ares, God of War, and was killed by Cadmus, who was later turned into a serpent by Ares as revenge for the death of his dragon offspring.

"Kadmos sent his henchmen forth to find a spring of living water. There stood an ancient forest undefiled by axe or saw, and in its heart a cave close-veiled in boughs and creepers, with its rocks joined in a shallow arch, and gushing out a wealth of water. Hidden in the cave there dwelt a

Snake, the Snake of Ares, with a crest that shone gleaming gold; its eyes flashed fire; its whole body was big with venom, and between its triple rows of teeth its three-forked tongue flickered. The Tyrians reached the forest glade on their ill-fated quest and dipped their sacs into the water. The frightful hiss of the serpent struck fear in them and they quaked in shock and terror. As it rose to its full height, it measured the length of the air and all the forest around. At once it grabbed the men who were frozen with fear or running for their lives.

"Every man of them it slew, with fangs that struck or coils that crushed. When Kadmos heard the hiss of death, he took his iron tipped lance and his mail of lion's skin and went to avenge the deaths of his friends.

"Now the dragon raged with foaming mouth and poison fangs bared. Its breath was like the black stink from holes of Stygia. Kadmos sent his javelin like a missile into the belly of the dragon, for all the rest of the beast was heavily armored to shield it. It sunk deep into the black carapace and pinned the beast against a mighty oak that labored under the weight until finally the dragon's blood spilled onto the grass and he was no more."

Gigantes: Some accounts give these children of Gaia the body of a man and the legs of a serpent, but earlier accounts liken them to hoplites, fully armored man-sized children formed of the earth who were the keepers of volcanoes and earthquakes. Their most notable place in Greek mythology is in the Gigantomachy, a war between the Giants and all the other Immortals including Titans, Olympians, and demi-gods.

Graea: These were two sea spirits often depicted as old crones (possibly three by some accounts) who were believed to share one tooth and one eye. They are the same crones who revealed the location of the Gorgons to Perseus. They are also seen as sirens with the head and arms of a woman and the body of a swan.

Griffin (Gryphon): This creature had the body of a lion and the head of an eagle, with eagle's talons on its front feet. The Griffin was believed to be the guardian of the divine; a majestic and powerful king of all beasts.

"And when the Gryfon roamed the wilderness on its winged course, it coveted the treasure of the Moirae and pursued by stealth, taking the priceless gold from the wakeful custody of the ones who guarded it.

Harpies: These were flying creatures with the head and body of a woman and the wings and claws of a bird, sometimes included as the guardians of the Gates of Hades.

Hippocampi: This creature was a great seahorse with the head and body of a horse and the tail of fish.

Hydra: This one-hundred-headed water snake was slain in the Second Labor of Hercules.

Lamia: The Lamia was a flying child eating monster with the body of woman, the wings and talons of a bird, and the tail of serpent with removable eyes.

Medusa the Gorgon: This was a female monster with snakes growing from its head, wings and claws. She was capable of turning men to stone with her gaze and was one of three, the offspring of Typhon and Echidna, who was killed by the hero, Perseus.

"Athena flew swiftly down from Mount Olympus and gave Perseus her dazzling shield of brass so that he might use it to reflect the image of mad Medusa. As he entered the gray land of the monster, he knew that she was the only one of the three that was not immortal, and he must slay her without looking at her. He crept into her lair while she slept and struck off her head by looking into the shield."

Poseidon was particularly interested in the affections of the strikingly lovely Medusa as solace after being rejected by the virgin goddess

Athena, so he took revenge by consorting with Medusa in Athena's temple, an act over which the goddess became furious. Athena in turn took her revenge by punishing Medusa; she turned her into a repulsive monster with thrashing snakes for hair.

Mermaids and Mermen: These were sea creatures, half man (or woman) and half fish who were known to be evil or kind.

Minotaur (Minotauros): This half-man half-bull monster lived in the Labyrinth (maze) created for King Minos by Daedalus, a craftsman and the father of Icarus. It was slain by Theseus who volunteered to kill the beast in order to stop the human sacrifices that were laid before it.

"The beast was ill-tempered and as strong as a bull, but with the cunning reason of a man and without graces, who sought only destruction and lustful vengeance, for even Daedalus, who contrived the maze, feared for his own life; he became confused upon the labyrinth's completion and spent many days working his way round and about to the doorway. And so the Minotaur was contained in this same confusion."

Pegasus and Chrysaor: These were the two unicorns that sprang from the neck of Medusa when she was killed by the hero, Perseus. These animals resembled a large horse and boar and were possessed of great wisdom. Unicorns are white and have a single horn growing from the forehead. Pegasus and Perseus saved Andromeda from the Kraken and this unicorn became the pet of the Goddess Athena, who later gave him as a gift to the Muses. Chrysaor later became the father of the three-bodied monster, Geryon, slain by Heracles in the Tenth Labor.

Phoenix: Phoenix of Assyria was the sacred bird who lived for five hundred years, died and then rose from the ashes to begin anew. It is said to be of golden feathers tinged with flames of red which emitted pure sunlight.

"The bird built a nest in which was the power of regeneration, of the oils of balsam and myrrh, and the tears of frankincense and other spices, at Helios where he buried his father in the temple, sitting on it and committing himself to the flames. When five long centuries have passed, he rises to the lofty heights and lines his nest; cinnamon, spikenard and spicy perfumes to ease his father's body to be reborn."

"... and, so embowered in spicy perfumes, ends his life's long span. Then from his father's body is reborn a little Phoenix to live the same long years. When time has built his strength with power to raise the weight, he lifts the nest--the nest his cradle and his father's tomb--as love and duty prompt, from that tall palm and carries it across the sky to reach the Sun's great city [Heliopolis in Egypt], and before the doors of the Sun's holy temple lays it down." (Ovid, Metamorphoses 15. 385 ff (trans. Melville) (Roman epic C1st B.C. to C1st A.D.)

Pythia: This python-dragon guarded the Oracle of Delphi and was slain by Apollo.

"Python guarded the sacred ground, which was Ge's (Mother Earth) circle of truth, regarded as the birth canal of the world. Apollo, son of Zeus, stood in the noon light and stared down the serpent. He drew an arrow from his quiver and placed it calmly in the bow. In an instant, the dragon's blood covered the ground. One after another until all his arrows were spent, he let them fly at the beast until finally it lay lifeless on the soil of truth. The faithful guardian of the sacred ground was felled by serene Apollo, the God of Truth and Prophecy, who would from then on be the ruler of Delphi and would dwell in this sanctuary."

Satyr: The beast was a man with the ears, tail, legs and horns of a goat and was closely associated with Pan.

Scylla: A six-headed creature who was once a beautiful girl, she was turned into a monster by an enchantress. The beast had long snake-like necks and dogs' heads growing from her back. She featured in Jason's voyage home along with Charybdis.

Sphinx: This creature had the body of lion and the head of woman. She would lay in wait for strangers on their way to Thebes and would not let them pass unless they were able to solve a riddle she would give to them. If they could not solve the riddle, she would kill them.

"The ruthless Spinx was unaware of the cleverness of Oedipus, was not afraid and asked for the riddle.

"What animal goes on four feet in the morning, two feet at noon and three feet in the evening?" it asked.

"Man," he responded, who crawls on all fours in infancy, the stands on two legs and finally, leaning on his crooked cane, has three legs."

The Sphinx flew into a mad rage for no mortal was ever able to outwit her. He threw herself over a cliff and died, and for this, Oedipus was made a hero."

There were also many magical mythical places believed by the ancients to exist.

Hyperborea: Hyperborea was a place beyond the noble mountains, far removed from the center of the world – Greece – at the northern rim of the flat circular disc that was Earth. Hyperborea was inaccessible to everyone except the Immortals, and this was a place without disease or aging, without war or suffering.

"There, grottos are pure ecstasy which sends forth the north wind and cools the people of Hellas (Greece); where the land is bright and golden, where gardens glow and the wind calms to sleep."

Elysian Plain: At the western edge of the earth was the Elysian Plain, also called the Fortunate Fields and the Isle of the Blessed, a place where mortals who were favored by the gods were transported. It was a heaven of sorts, but not the same heaven personified by Ouranos or Kronos. It was a joyful place where mortals would enjoy an immortality of bliss without knowing the pain of death. It was still the domain of the God Hades, Lord of the Underworld, but in contrast to Tartaros where death, disease and ghosts endlessly tormented the souls of those who lived an evil life, and where sunshine never entered, the Elysian Plain was beautiful and vibrant, illuminated by sunshine and stars.

The River Styx: Styx was named for the Naiad Styx, or she was the embodiment of the river, whose name means "hateful". Styx the Naiad was responsible for helping the Olympians defeat the Giants in the Gigantomachy, and for this she was honored by Zeus by being made the most holy and sacred river. But this only pertained to the gods; the water was lethal to mortals, however this was the river into which

Achilles' mother dipped him to protect him in battle.

"Then the Goddess Themis prophesied that she [Thetis, the Nereid] would bear a son mightier than his father, Zeus, and so she became the wife of Peleus and mother of Achilles. And she took the babe to the river and immersed him in the magical waters.

"Styx was older than the gods, being the oldest child of Oceanus and Tethys, and was dark, laying herself outside the Gates of Hades. And her waters could break through iron, yet one alone was saved by her deadly power, by Thetis who knew the water's secrets.

"And so it was she dipped him carefully in the dark river to make him invincible. And Achilles grew strong and was a man of war, protected through long and arduous battles by the waters of the holy river, until a poisonous arrow struck his heel where his mother's hand had held him, and so was not protected by the river and it killed him."

There was also a much smaller body of water, a spring, called Styx that had the miraculous quality of determining virginity.

Chapter 10: The Constellations

Those gods, goddesses, semi-divine creatures and mortals who played an important role were given the honor of being made into stars or constellations of stars, where their spirits would be seen forever in the heavenly night sky. They are considered the sixth class of immortals. Each constellation is possessed of the spirit of a legendary being who was either cursed or favored by the gods.

Andromeda (The Princess): The daughter of Queen Cassiopeia who boasted of her beauty and angered Poseidon and sacrificed her daughter to the Sea Monster to appease the God of the Sea. Andromeda was saved by Perseus who killed the beast by showing him the head of Medusa. Andromeda is the great grandmother of Heracles.

Aquila (The Eagle): Aquila is a lesser known constellation, the eagle who is the keeper of the lightning bolts of Zeus.

Ara (The Altar): During a battle between the Titans and the Olympians, the Cyclopes who had been saved by Zeus from Tartarus built an altar and burned a sacrifice so that the smoke would hide Zeus and his brothers as they attacked Cronus and the Titans. In gratitude, Zeus placed the altar in the sky at the horizon, under the Milky Way which now appears to be the rising smoke.

Argo Navis (The Ship): The *Argo* is the ship which carried Jason and the Argonauts on their adventures.

Aries (The Ram): The golden ram was sent by Hera to help the children of Nephele, a cloud which Zeus had disguised as the Goddess Hera. This is the same ram whose fleece was later sought by Jason and the Arogonauts.

Auriga (The Charioteer): Erichthonius was the son of Hephaestus, born with the lower body of a snake on whom Athena took pity and raised the boy.

He often honored her and was eventually placed in the sky as a reward.

Boötes (The Bear Chaser): This is Icarius, the wine cultivator, who was shown favor by Dionysus by placing him and his dog, Maera, in the sky. Maera is the start Procyon in Canis Minor.

Cancer (The Crab): This the same crab who distracted Heracles as he fought the Hydra. Since Hera hated Heracles, the crab was rewarded with a place in the sky.

Canis Major (The Greater Dog): This is one of the dogs that belonged to Orion, the hunter. When Orion was killed by the scorpion, the dogs were placed in the sky beside him.

Cassiopeia (The Queen): She believed herself to be more beautiful than the nymphs of Poseidon, who punished her by demanding she sacrifice her daughter to the Kraken. The legends say that she and her husband, King Cepheus, must stand foot to foot in the heavens so they can never speak to one another. As an added punishment, Cassiopeia is not permitted to set below the surface of the sea (as seen from northern latitudes because of her insults to the nymphs.

Centaurus (The Centaur): Chiron was the kindly Centaur who was accidentally killed by the poison arrows of Heracles. He voluntarily took the place of Prometheus on the rock so that only one of them would suffer, and for this he was rewarded with a place among the stars.

Cepheus (The King): This is the husband of Casseopeia, who was part of the fallout between his wife's vanity and the wrath of Poseidon. He was also one of the Argonauts.

Cetus (The Sea Monster): This monster is a sibling of the Gorgons, Cerberus, the Chimera, and the Hydra.

Corona Borealis (The Northern Crown): The seven stars in the crown constellation represent the seven maidens and seven youths that had been sacrificed to the Minotaur. The crown was a gift from Hephaestus to Ariadne, wife of Theseus, for helping him get out of the Labyrinth.

Cygnus (The Swan): Phaëthon, son of Helios, died when he fell out of the chariot of the Sun and into the River Eridanus. His brother Cygnus repeatedly dove in search of him and the gods later transformed him into a swan.

Delphinus (The Dolphin): Poseidon tried to convince one of the Nereids, Amphirite, to marry him. He sent a dolphin to plead his case and she finally agreed to be his bride. The dolphin was rewarded with a place in the sky.

Draco (The Dragon): This is the same dragon that protected the golden apples and the Golden Fleece.

Eridanus (The River): This is the river into which Phaëthon, son of Helios fell when he lost control of the horses who pulled the chariot.

Gemini (The Twins): The fraternal twins Castor and Pollux were born of Leda, a mortal, but Pollux was fathered by Zeus and was immortal, while Castor's father was a mortal, Tyndareus. When Castor was killed in the Olympic games, Pollux asked to die also so they would not be separated, and Zeus placed them together in the sky.

Heracles (The Hero): Hercules earned his position in the sky by performing many acts of bravery. He is a son of Zeus and Alcmene, a mortal, the granddaughter of Perseus and Andromeda.

Hydra (The Multi-Headed Monster): One of the monsters killed by Hercules, which had one immortal head.

Leo (The Lion): This was Hera's Nemean lion killed by Heracles as one of his 12 Labors. He wore the skin as a trophy and Hera set her courageous lion in the sky so his bravery against the mighty Heracles would be remembered forever.

Lepus (The Rabbit): The original rabbit imported to Leros, where the breed was finally exterminated after infesting the land. The gods placed the hare in the sky as a reminder.

Lupus (The Wolf): The she-wolf is sometimes said to be the lover of the God Apollo, and at other times the lover of the Centaur, but it's shown in the sky as being impaled on a spear by the Centaur.

Lyra (The Harp): The God Apollo invented the lyre and gave it to the God to Orpheus who was married to Eurydice. When she died, he used the lyre to subdue the hounds of hell and rescue his beloved from the realm of the dead. When Orpheus died, Zeus place his lyre in the heavens.

Milky Way (The Galaxy): Before Cronus swallowed the rock he believed to be the baby Zeus, he asked Rhea to nurse it and when she pressed the rock against her bosom, the spurting milk became the Milky Way.

Ophiuchus (The   Physician):

Asclepius (Ophiuchus) was a great physician raised by the centaur Chiron. Because he could bring the dead back to life, Hades had Zeus strike him with a thunderbolt and kill him. Zeus then regretted his deed and instead made Ophiuchus immortal by giving him a place among the stars.

Orion (The Hunter): Orion was a giant hunter who died while in the service of the Goddess Artemis. The legend tells us that Zeus sent the scorpion to kill him and they both died in the battle. This is why we see Orion in the winter sky and Scorpius in the summer sky, so they can no longer fight.

Other accounts of Orion's death and occultation tell us that he was killed by Artemis herself as he walked in the sea, for she mistook him for a bobbing thing and drew to the challenge of hitting it with her arrow. When she discovered it was her beloved Orion, she set him among the stars.

Pegasus (The   Winged   Horse): Pegasus is the famed winged mount of Perseus.

Pisces (The Fishes): Typhon was in love with the Goddess Aphrodite and in order to hide from him and protect her, she and her son Eros were turned into fishes. To show their appreciation, fishes were placed among the stars.

Pleiades (The Sisters): (Whose name means "flock of doves"). These were the daughters of Atlas and Pleione, an Oceanid, who were chased by Orion the Hunter for seven years. To help them escape, Zeus turned them into doves and placed them in the sky just to the west of Orion where he can see them, but never catch up to them.

There were seven Pleiades:

Maia – Mother; Nurse

Alcyone - Queen who wards off evil

Electra – Amber; Shining; Bright

Celaino - Swarthy

Taygete - Long-necked

Sterope/Asterope   –   Lightening;
Twinkling; Sun-face

Merope – Eloquent; Mortal; Bee-eater

Sagitta (The Arrow): This is the arrow shot by Heracles when he killed the vulture that pecked at the liver of Prometheus.

Sagittarius (The Archer): This is the archer, Crotus the Centaur, son of the God Pan and the nymph, Euphyme. He was raised with the nine Muses, daughters of Zeus and Mnemosyne. The Muses asked Zeus to honor him with a constellation.

Scorpius (The Scorpion): When Orion began hunting too many of Gaia's animals, she sent the scorpion to battle him. They both died in the battle and Zeus maintained peace in the heavens by placing the hunter in the winter and the beast in the summer so they are unable to view each other.

Taurus (The Bull): There are many bulls which feature in Greek mythology. This one is the bull Zeus turned himself into when he kidnapped Europa, who bore King Minos by him.

Ursa Major (The Greater Bear): This is Callisto, the beautiful lover of Zeus who was almost killed by Arcas, her son by Zeus, who saw her as the bear which she had been turned into by Hera.

Ursa Minor (The Lesser Bear): Arcas is the son of Zeus and Callisto, who was changed into a bear along with his mother. Both were placed in the sky.

Virgo (The Young Maiden): This is the chaste Goddess Demeter whose daughter Persephone was made to live in Hades part of the year. Virgo appears in the spring sky when Persephone is returned to her mother from Hades.

The Eight Class of Immortals

Still there was another class of immortals, the eighth class. These were the heroes who were worshipped after death and were considered minor divinities. They often began their lives as mortals, and included Achilles (Akhilleus), Theseus and Perseus, Alkmene, Helene and Baubo, Kings Erikhthonios, Kadmos, and Pelops.

Afterword

It's easy to confuse many of the names and timelines of Greek mythology. The ancient writings of Hesiod, Plutarch, Homer, and other pre-Socratic philosophers are frustratingly unclear in terms of which came first, the chicken or the egg, and as is always the case with ancient text, transliterations are often simply wrong or out of context.

But the stories they have given us elucidate our look into the rich history of Ancient Greece and her neighbors, the imaginative stories created about what they believed to be the origins of their world, the gods and goddesses, and the heroes and monsters that featured prominently in their daily lives.

Men who could perform seemingly impossible feats, such as Heracles and Perseus, were the hope of the people when the gods seemed too impossible to please, and each tale and adventure personifies all of man's flaws, fallacies, goodness, strength, hope, and courage. Many of these stories are still well-known today, for a good story never dies. Though the Immortals of Olympus are extinct, they live on through great literature and poetry, both ancient and modern. They hold their place because they are the material substance of some of the finest productions of art, and the stars are there to bear witness to the great deeds and eternal power of the Gods of Ancient Greece.

Appendix I: Mythological Greek Divinities by Association

Theoi is the ancient Greek work for 'gods'. There is often more than one deity with the same name and other entities such as nymphs, for example, which take on the names of gods, but the affiliations below are the basic order of groups as they appear in the ancient texts. You will also find that some deities appear to have parents who are also their children and vice versa, and some who appear later in "history" but are also written as haven been born earlier.

Primordial Deities:

Aether – Upper Air

Ananke – Necessity

Atropos – Cutter (Fate who is the cutter of the thread of one's life at the predetermined time of death)

Chaos - Void

Chronos – Time

Clotho – Spinner (Fate who is the spinner of the Thread of one's life)

Erebus - Darkness

Eros – Sexuality; Desire

Ge – Earth (Gaia)

Hemera - Day

Lachesis – Apportioner (Fate who measures out the thread of one's life)

Nyx - Night

Ouranos – Dome of the Sky

Tartarus - Pit

Thalassa - Sea

Titan Deities:

Titanes (Males)

Coeus – God of Intelligence who presided over the axis of heaven

Crius – God of Leadership, Mastery and the Constellations

Hyperion – God of Light; father of Helios (Sun), Selene (Moon), Eos (Dawn)

Iapetus – God of Mortality

Kronos – God of Time; later interpreted from the primordial Chronos as *tempora quae sicut falx in se recurrunt* meaning 'as the foliage season which is recurrent';

Oceanus – God of Earth-encircling Fresh Water Rivers

Ophioneus (Ophion) – Little is written about Ophion; an early rival of Kronus for control of the world

Titanides (Females)

Dione – Mother of Aphrodite by Zeus; she presided over the Oracle at Dodona

Eurybia – Goddess of the Power of the Sea

Mnemosyne – Goddess of Memory, Words and Language; Mother of the Nine Muses

Phoebe – Goddess of Bright Intellect and the Oracle of Delphi

Rhea – Goddess of Female Fertility and Mountain Wilderness

Tethys – Goddess of the Subterranean Sources of Fresh Water;

Theia – Goddess of Sight and Clear Blue Skies; Mother of Helios, Selene and Eos

Themis – Goddess of Divine Law and Natural Order

Hyperionides

Eos – Goddess of the Dawn

Helios – God of the Sun

Selene – Goddess of the Moon

Koionides

Asteria – Goddess of Nocturnal Rites

Aura – Goddess of the Breeze

Lelantos – God of the Unseen and Stalking Prey

Leto – Goddess of Motherhood

Krionides

Astraeus – God of the Stars; Father of the spirits of the Four Winds by Eos

Pallas – God of Warcraft; Father of Victory, Power, Force, and Rivalry

Perses – God of Destruction and Laying Waste

Iapetionedes

Atlas – God of Daring condemned to carry the Dome of Heaven on his shoulders

Epimetheus – God of Afterthought

Menoetius – God of Rash Anger

Prometheus – God of Forethought; Creator of Mankind

Okeanides

Clymene – Goddess of Fame and Infamy; wife of Iapetu

Eurynome – Goddess of the Water Pasture; Mother of the Charites by Zeus

Metis – Goddess of Good Counsel; Daughter of Athena

Styx – Goddess of the underworld river, Styx

Olympian Deities

Dodekathion

Aphrodite – Goddess of Love, Beauty and Intercourse born of sea-foam around the castrated genitals of Uranus

Apollo – God of Prophecy, Music and Healing

Ares – God of War and Bloodshed

Artemis – Goddess of Hunting, Wild Animals, Children, and Childbirth

Athena – Goddess of War and Skilled Crafts

Demeter – Goddess of Agriculture and the Fertile Earth

Dionysus – God of Wine and Festivity

Hephaestus – God of Fire, Volcanism and Smiths

Hera – Air; Goddess of Heaven, Women and Marriage

Hermes – God of Animal Husbandry, Fertility of the Herds, Trade, Messengers, Merchants, Travel, and Athletes

Hestia – Goddess of Hearth and Home

Poseidon – God of the Sea, Horses, Rivers, and Earthquakes

Zeus – God of the Heavens, Weather, Fate, and Kings

Theoi Olympioi

Asclepius – God of Medicine

Deimos – The Daemon of Terror

Eileithyia – Goddess of Childbirth

Enyo – Goddess of War

Eris – Goddess of Strife and Discord

Eros – God of Love

Hebe – Goddess of Youth

Heracles – Ascended to Olympus after the 12 Labors; The Protector of Man; considered the greatest of the Greek heroes

Harmonia – Goddess of Harmony and Unity

Iris – Goddess of the Rainbow

Paean – Physician of the Gods

Pan – God of Shepherds and Goatherds

Pandia – Goddess of Brightness

Phobos – Daemon of Fear

Mousai (Muses)

Calliope – Epic Poetry

Clio – History

Erato – Love Poetry

Euterpe – Lyric Poetry

Melpomene - Tragedy

Polyhymnia - Hymns

Terpsichore – Choral Dance and Song

Thalia - Comedy

Urania - Astronomy

Charites (Graces)

Aglaea – Goddess of Beauty

Euphrosyne – Goddess of Mirth and Merriment

Thalia – Goddess of Festive Good Cheer

Horae (Hours)

Bia – Goddess of Force

Dike (Dice) – Goddess of Justice

Eirene – Goddess of Peace

Eunomia – Goddess of Good Order and spring Pastures

Kratos – God of War

Nike – Goddess of Victory

Zelos – God of Rivalry and Envy

Oceanic Deities

Theoi Halioi

Amphitrite – Goddess Queen of the Sea; a Nereide

Ceto – Goddess of the Dangers of the Sea

Nereus – Father of the fifty Nereides; God of the Sea

Oceanus – God of the Earth-encircling fresh water river, Oceanus

Phorcys – A sea god; father of sea monsters

Poseidon – King of the Sea; God of Horses, Rivers and Earthquakes

Proteus – A sea god; Herdsman of the Seals of Poseidon

Tethys – Goddess of Subterranean Sources of Fresh Water

Thalassa (Pontus) – Goddess of the Sea

Thetis - Goddess and leader of the Nereides; Mother of Achilles

Triton – The God of Calm Seas

Oceanids

Clymene – Goddess of Fame and Infamy

Dione – Goddess of the Oracle of Dodona

Doris – Goddess of Fresh Water mingling with the Brine

Eurynome – Goddess of Water Pasture; Mother of the Charites by Zeus

Metis – A Naiad of the River Meles

Nemesis – Goddess of Indignation and Undeserved Fortune

Pleione – A nymph; wife of Atlas pursued by Orion

Tyche – Goddess of Good Fortune and Luck

Nereides

Amphitrite – Goddess Queen of the Sea

Galatea – One of the fifty Nereides

Thetis – Goddess and leader of the Nereides; Mother of Achilles

Potamoi

Achelous – God of the River Aetolia

Asopus – God of the Rivers Boeotia and Argos

Enipeus – God of the River Enipeus

Scamander – God of the River Scamander in Troy

Chthonic Deities

Theoi Khthonioi

Demeter – Goddess of Agriculture and the Fertile Earth

Gaia – Primeval Mother Earth

Hades – God of the Dead; King of the Underworld

Hecate – Goddess of Witchcraft, Ghosts and Necromancy

Persephone – Goddess of Spring; Daughter of Demeter; Part-time Queen of the Underworld

Erinyes (Furies)

Adikia –Goddess of Injustice

Alecto – Constant Anger

Megaera – The Jealous

Tisiphone – Avenger of Murder

Earthborn

Cyclopes – Three one-eyed giants of Uranus and Gaia

Gigantes - The giants of Greek myth which included beings like the Aloedae, Typhon, Antaeus, Charybdis, Orion, Tityus, the Cyclopes, and the Hecatonkcheires

Hecatonkcheires – Fifty-headed hundred-handed giants born of Uranus and Gaia

Kouretes – Spirits (Diamones) who guarded the infant Zeus

Typhon – The monstrous storm daemon

Apotheothenai

Aeacus – One of the three judges of the underworld

Iacchus – God of Processions

Minos - A mortal appointed judge of the dead of the underworld

Rhadamanthys – Lord of the Island of the Blessed; One of the three judges of the underworld

Triptolemus – God of Sowing and Threshing Grain

Trophonius – A man swallowed up by the earth and transformed into an oracular daemon

Appendix II: Orders of Nymphs

Anigrides: Healer nymphs.

Dodonides or Dododaean: These were the nymphs who brought up Zeus.

Dryades: Nymphs of the Forest, the hunting companions of Artemis.

Epimeliades: Protectors of Sheep.

Haliai: Sea nymphs. Haliai comes from the word for *sea*.

Heliades or Heliadai: Daughters of Helios, the Sun; the sisters of Phaeton: Aegle, Aetheria, Dioxippe, and Merope, who were turned into poplar trees and whose tears were changed into amber.

Hespirides: There were the nymphs who guarded the Tree of the Golden Apples stolen by Herakles in his Eleventh Labor.

Lamusidean: These were the nurses of Dionysus who were driven mad by Hera.

Maliades: These dryads embodied fruit trees.

Naiades: These were the nymphs of freshwater streams rivers and lakes. They were the daughters of river gods. There were 5 types of Naiades:

Pegaiai: the Nymphs of Springs

Krinaia, the Nymphs of Fountains

Potameides, the Nymphs of Rivers and Streams

Limnades or Limnatides, the Nymphs of Lakes

Eleionomai, the Nymphs of Marshes

Napaea: These were the Nymphs of the Valley. In Greek *nape* means dell.

Nereides: The 50 daughters of Nereus (the Sea; Poseidon), one of whom was Amphitrite, his wife.

Nyseides: The nymphs that lived on Mount Nysa and raised the young Dionysus.

Oceanids: There were allegedly 3000 Oceanids, the children of the Titans Tethys and Oceanus.

Oreades: Nymphs of the Mountains; Echo, for example, the nymph who pursued Narcissus.

Thriai: Bee-Nymphs who raised Apollo and who used honey to make prophesies.